In late 1940 the War Office's Department of Tank Design (1) issued a preliminary specification for a new cruiser tank as a replacement for the Crusader, which was at that time being prepared to serve with the regiments of the Royal Armoured Corps in North Africa. The order called for a much more heavily protected tank with armour thicknesses of 65mm on the hull front and 75mm for the turret. The new tank was to be armed with the Ordnance Quick-Firing (OQF) 6pdr gun which had itself been in development since 1938 when it was realised that the standard anti-tank gun of the period, the 2pdr, would not be adequate to deal with the next generation of German tanks.

Both Vauxhall Motors and the Birmingham Railway Carriage and Wagon Company (BRCW) offered designs for the new tank but it was decided that Nuffield Mechanisation and Aero, which had manufactured the Crusader, would undertake production of what was by now designated A24 Cruiser Mk VII.

In January 1941 six pilot models were ordered and these were to be fitted with Nuffield's 410hp Liberty engine. At the same time Leyland Motors and Rolls-Royce had been co-operating on the development of an un-supercharged version of the highly successful Merlin aircraft engine for use in an armoured vehicle. The result was the Meteor, a twelve-cylinder motor capable of 600hp, offering a significant increase in power over the Liberty which had in fact changed little from the original design first introduced into service during the 1914-18 war. The Meteor had been tested in a modified Crusader in early 1941 and the results were so impressive that it was immediately decided that the new engine would be adopted for the A24 project (2).

However, the Meteor would available in quantity for some tin was accepted that A24 productio have to go ahead, initially leasᴛ, wɪᴛʜ the Nuffield Liberty engine. As late as September 1941 design and development of the new cruiser was proceeding along two quite distinct paths with Nuffields producing their Liberty-engined A24 and BRCW working on the Meteor-powered version. In addition, the BRCW variant had replaced the problematic Wilson transmission with a Merritt-Brown model, a much-improved suspension and a revised cooling system and was given the new designation of A27 Cruiser Mk VIII (3). Somewhat confusingly, both tanks retained the name Cromwell.

By this time the Nuffield A24 design was exhibiting so many teething problems that the War Office felt it necessary to reduce the number ordered. In the meantime the BRCW prototype had completed its initial trials with some success and it was decided that the main effort would be diverted to the A27 programme. However, the production of the Rolls-Royce engines proceeded slowly and it was necessary to fit a number of A27 tanks with the Nuffield Liberty. These were assembled by Leyland and designated A27L while BRCW Meteor-powered tanks were referred to as A27M. This meant that by the summer of 1942 three versions of the Cromwell tank were simultaneously under development and in an effort to alleviate some of the resulting confusion, the War Office ordered that the Nuffield, Leyland and BRCW tanks be referred to initially as Cromwell I, II and III and later as A24 Cruiser Mk VII Cavalier, A27L Cruiser Mk VIII Centaur and A27M Cruiser Mk VIII Cromwell respectively (4).

committee made up of manufacturers, government officials, service personnel and other interested parties, which met weekly.

2. With a typical lack of urgency the Tank Board ordered that full-scale production of the Meteor begin 'relatively early'.

3. Engine overheating had been a major problem with the Crusader, particularly in the desert, caused largely by altering the Liberty Mk III to fit the tank's cramped engine compartment.

4. The design differences of the Cromwell and Centaur, although minor, were not limited to the engine and are discussed in the Technical section which begins on page 59.

Engine fitters examine a Meteor engine at a training facility in Britain in early 1944. The tank is a Cromwell Mk I which has been relegated to an instructional role. Of note are the early perforated road wheels.

Photographed in the early hours of 6 June 1944, this Centaur is one of two vehicles from 4th Battery, 2nd Armoured Support Regiment, Royal Marine Armoured Support Group that took part in the assault on the German strongpoint WN-26 at Langrune-sur-Mer. Just visible behind the soldier in the left background is the other tank which was disabled after losing a track to German mines.

Notes

1. The penetrative power of the 6pdr was in fact slightly superior to the US 75mm gun but its high-explosive ammunition was almost useless.

By 1943 those Cavaliers that had been completed were relegated to a training role or used as Artillery Observation Post (AOP) tanks. In addition, it was decided that production would continue on the Centaur and Cromwell until sufficient Meteor engines were available, at which time the Centaur would be phased out of production. Indeed, by this time the Centaur's main function was seen by the War Office as providing hulls which could be used in future Cromwell production.

During the fighting in North Africa and Sicily, the British army's experience with the US M4 medium tank had shown the efficacy of the dual-purpose 75mm gun which, in addition to its anti-tank capability, could fire an effective high-explosive round and a suitably re-bored version of the 6pdr, the Ordnance ROQF 75mm gun, was incorporated into the A27 production schedule (1). The resulting vehicle was referred to as the Cromwell IV and was the most numerous variant produced with almost 2,000 vehicles leaving the assembly lines. But in the same way that development and manufacturing delays dogged the installation of the Meteor engine, sufficient quantities of the new 75mm weapons would not be available for some time and both the Centaur and Cromwell continued to be assembled with 6pdr guns. In fact, none of the 75mm-armed Centaur III tanks manufactured went into combat, although over 200 were built, and as we shall see AOP Centaurs were fitted with dummy guns and the tanks of the Royal Marines were all armed with 95mm howitzers.

The first tanks were issued to the regiments of 9th Armoured Division between April and September 1943 and while the Cromwell was regarded favourably, the divisional commander,

the highly experienced Major-General John Conyers D'Arcy, believed that it would be 'criminal' to regard the Centaur as anything other than a stop-gap measure. Indeed, during these trials the Centaur proved to be as mechanically unreliable as the Crusader or the Covenanter, with which the division was equipped at the time, and production was again cut back. It was only through the influence of Lord Nuffield that development continued at all, even as both the Centaur and Cavalier were demoted to auxiliary roles, and production carried on until early 1945 with the last versions built as anti-aircraft tanks.

In February 1944 the Final Specification (FS) for what was referred to as the Battle Cromwell laid out the production features and necessary modifications which were considered essential for an active service vehicle. This document not only set out the type of engine and transmission that was to be fitted but also called for increased structural strength and further waterproofing. The Final Specification effectively made all production vehicles prior to the 75mm-armed Cromwell IV model obsolete.

On the eve of the Normandy invasion Cromwell gun tanks and Close Support (CS) variants had been allocated to the reconnaissance regiments of 11th and Guards Armoured Divisions and, except for thirty-six Firefly VC tanks, completely equipped the three regiments of 22nd Armoured Brigade of 7th Armoured Division in addition to the division's reconnaissance regiment. In training the crews had been impressed with the Cromwell's speed, reliability and the punch of its 75mm gun. But the real tests would come now, conducted in earnest on the battlefields of France, Holland and Germany.

Despite the indecision, political infighting and delays in production that characterised the development and introduction into service of the Cromwell, by June 1944 almost 400 vehicles, including close support and recovery tanks, were on hand with the regiments of the Royal Armoured Corps (RAC). This figure does not include the more than sixty Cromwells of all types allocated to the 1st Polish Armoured Division or the Centaurs operated by the Royal Marines. Unfortunately, accurate figures are not available for the number or exact types of OP tanks issued to the regimental headquarters units and batteries of the Royal Artillery and this would also have included modified Centaurs and Cavaliers. Although the armoured reconnaissance regiments were controlled by the RAC they are include under a separate heading. Note that they are not listed in order of precedence but rather in an arrangement that benefits the narrative. Also, I have chosen to describe most battles and operations briefly as they were examined in the earlier titles in the TankCraft series, *Sherman Tanks: British Army and Royal Marines Normandy Campaign 1944* and *Churchill Tanks: British Army North-west Europe 1944-1945*. Not included in this study are details of the 10th Polish Mounted Rifles Regiment, the armoured reconnaissance regiment of 1st Polish Armoured Division, and the regiments of the 1st (Czechoslovakian) Independent Armoured Brigade Group, although the colourful markings used by those units are depicted in the Camouflage and Markings section.

22nd Armoured Brigade. Attached to 7th Armoured Division, the famous Desert Rats, this brigade was made up of regiments that had served with the division in North Africa, Sicily and Italy. This was the only British armoured brigade equipped, in the main, with the Cromwell tank. Each troop was supposed to be supported by a 17pdr-armed Sherman Firefly although 1st RTR actually had one more than its official allocation of these powerful tanks on hand in June 1944 (1).

Elements of the brigade first arrived in Normandy on Thursday, 8 June 1944 and at that time 22nd Armoured Brigade contained 1st Royal Tank Regiment (RTR), 5th RTR and 4th County of London Yeomanry. As the campaign wore on and supplies became available, the brigade's total of Fireflies rose from thirty-six in June to sixty-seven by December 1944.

On 13 June 1944, during the fighting that took place in and around the town of Villers-Bocage, 4th County of London Yeomanry was so badly mauled that it was amalgamated with 3rd County of London Yeomanry and the resulting composite regiment remained with 4th Armoured Brigade for the duration of the campaign, referred to as 3rd/4th County of London Yeomanry.

In late July 1944, 5th Royal Inniskilling Dragoon Guards (2) joined the brigade to replace the Yeomanry regiment and as the Iniskillings were senior to both the RTR battalions a reorganisation was required

Notes

1. Although it is almost certain that the term Firefly was never applied to these tanks during the war I have continued to use it here as a matter of convenience.

2. As the regiment was originally raised from men from the town of Inniskillen in Northern Ireland it is referred to by that name in some accounts. Throughout this book I has used the names of regiments given in *Regulations for the Clothing of the Army* published in 1936 and the amendment issued in 1939.

Photographed on Gold Beach on 14 June 1944 this Cromwell Mk IV of 5th Royal Tank Regiment has been fitted with a complete set of deep wading equipment. The tank's WD Number, T187832, is displayed on the hull front, the turret wading stack and on the turret side above the name Satan's Chariot. A pin-up or painting of a young woman has been fixed to the right of the driver's position with waterproofing sealant. Note that the rear part of the sandshield has been inverted to provide extra stowage capacity, a modification more commonly seen on the Sherman tanks of 4th Armoured Brigade.

to accurately represent the order of precedence with a necessary change in arm of service markings (1).

During August the brigade took part in the battles for Mont Pincon and Saint-Pierre-la-Vielle, north-east of Vire, as part of the Allied effort to trap the retreating Germans. Elements of the brigade entered Lisieux, an important road junction almost exactly halfway between Caen and Rouen, on 23 August and advanced to the banks of the Seine by the end of the month.

Pushing through Belgium and across the Somme, the tanks of 22nd Armoured Brigade pressed on towards Ghent where a task force made up of the Inniskillings and 11th Hussars (Prince Albert's Own), the division's armoured car regiment,

captured the city on 5 September 1944.

The brigade was involved in the heavy fighting around the River Maas that began in late October and did not end until the first weeks of the new year.

In January 1945 the brigade took part in Operation Blackcock, the action to clear the west bank of the River Roer, and the subsequent crossing of the Rhine which began on 25 March. Fighting on their own soil the Germans offered fierce resistance and it was only with great difficulty that the towns of Ibbenburen, Wildehausen and Soltau were taken before the brigade could move on to Hamburg.

After the fall of the city forward elements of the division were able to penetrate as far as Kiel when the war ended on 8 May 1945.

Notes

1. The markings are explained in some detail in the Camouflage and Markings section of this book and also in the second book in the TankCraft series, *Sherman Tanks: British Army and Royal Marines Normandy Campaign 1944.*

ARMOURED BRIGADE, JUNE 1944

The diagram below shows an armoured brigade complete with infantry motor battalion and is based on War Establishment (WE) II/1031/1 of 30 November 1943. This type of formation was referred to as an Armoured Brigade Type A and the brigades of the three conventional armoured divisions that served in the 1944–45 campaign, the 7th, 11th and Guards, were all organised using this structure. Type B brigades lacked the infantry component and of the independent formations only 4th Armoured Brigade and 8th Armoured Brigade were formed as Type A units in 1944.

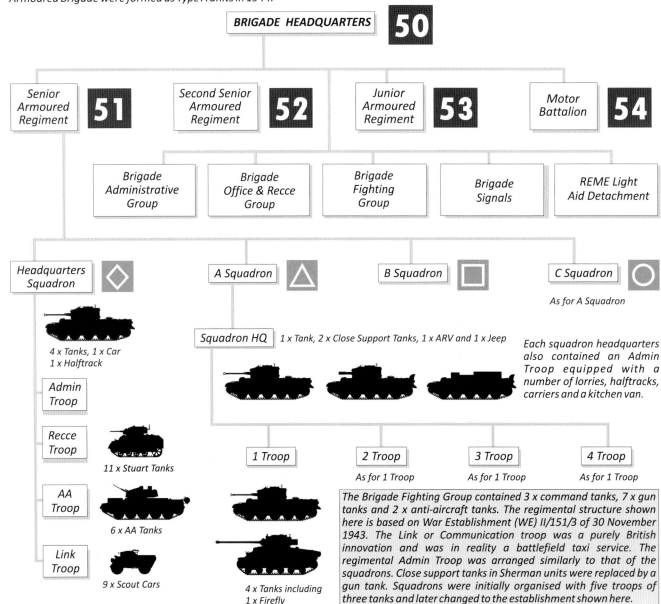

Photographed in Normandy during the during the advance towards Aunay-sur-Odon in late July 1944, this welded-hull Cromwell Mk VwD is from 1st RTR. Although heavily camouflaged, the WD number T121763W, the appliqué armour on the hull front and the commander's All Round Vision (ARV) cupola can be seen. Note also the additional wireless aerial on the turret side. In the original print the name Gladys is just visible above the driver's visor.

This Cromwell Mk IV, built on a Type C hull, was photographed on 18 July 1944, the first day of Operation Goodwood, crossing the Bailey bridge constructed over the Orne near Bénouville. Although the censor has done his best to obliterate the tank's markings the WD number T190031 identifies the unit as B Squadron, 1st Royal Tank Regiment. Note the name Diana on the hull locker and evidence of a white Allied recognition star on the open loader's hatch. This was the first Bailey bridge built in France and due to its impressive size was christened London Bridge.

1ST BATTALION, ROYAL TANK REGIMENT, JUNE 1944

Vehicle names were not left to the discretion of the crew, as they were in other armies, but were devised and approved at regimental or brigade command level. The names often followed a certain theme, for example the names of famous racehorses, and the most common practice was for names to begin with the squadron letter. Shown below are the tanks of 1st RTR at the beginning of the Normandy campaign. Note that the spelling, although sometimes questionable, is shown exactly as it appears in the regiment's records. Unfortunately no account exists of the names used by the regimental headquarters.

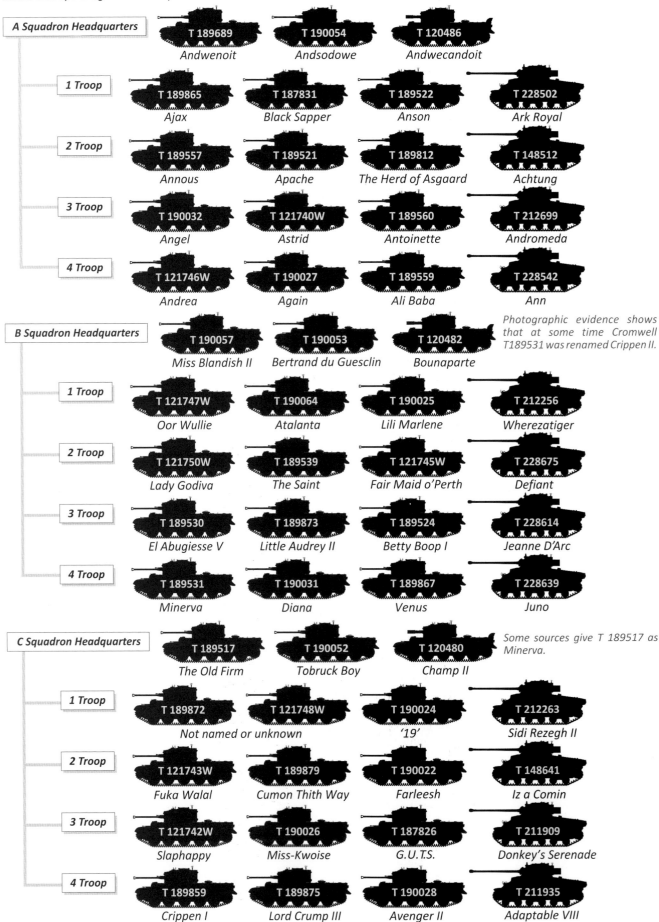

A Squadron Headquarters

| T 189689 | T 190054 | T 120486 |
| Andwenoit | Andsodowe | Andwecandoit |

1 Troop

| T 189865 | T 187831 | T 189522 | T 228502 |
| Ajax | Black Sapper | Anson | Ark Royal |

2 Troop

| T 189557 | T 189521 | T 189812 | T 148512 |
| Annous | Apache | The Herd of Asgaard | Achtung |

3 Troop

| T 190032 | T 121740W | T 189560 | T 212699 |
| Angel | Astrid | Antoinette | Andromeda |

4 Troop

| T 121746W | T 190027 | T 189559 | T 228542 |
| Andrea | Again | Ali Baba | Ann |

B Squadron Headquarters

| T 190057 | T 190053 | T 120482 |
| Miss Blandish II | Bertrand du Guesclin | Bounaparte |

Photographic evidence shows that at some time Cromwell T189531 was renamed Crippen II.

1 Troop

| T 121747W | T 190064 | T 190025 | T 212256 |
| Oor Wullie | Atalanta | Lili Marlene | Wherezatiger |

2 Troop

| T 121750W | T 189539 | T 121745W | T 228675 |
| Lady Godiva | The Saint | Fair Maid o'Perth | Defiant |

3 Troop

| T 189530 | T 189873 | T 189524 | T 228614 |
| El Abugiesse V | Little Audrey II | Betty Boop I | Jeanne D'Arc |

4 Troop

| T 189531 | T 190031 | T 189867 | T 228639 |
| Minerva | Diana | Venus | Juno |

C Squadron Headquarters

| T 189517 | T 190052 | T 120480 |
| The Old Firm | Tobruck Boy | Champ II |

Some sources give T 189517 as Minerva.

1 Troop

| T 189872 | T 121748W | T 190024 | T 212263 |
| Not named or unknown | | '19' | Sidi Rezegh II |

2 Troop

| T 121743W | T 189879 | T 190022 | T 148641 |
| Fuka Walal | Cumon Thith Way | Farleesh | Iz a Comin |

3 Troop

| T 121742W | T 190026 | T 187826 | T 211909 |
| Slaphappy | Miss-Kwoise | G.U.T.S. | Donkey's Serenade |

4 Troop

| T 189859 | T 189875 | T 190028 | T 211935 |
| Crippen I | Lord Crump III | Avenger II | Adaptable VIII |

This Cromwell Mk V is based on a Type E hull with applique armour and is believed to have been the sole example of a welded hull built by the English Electric Company. Although difficult to discern from this image, the turret may also be of welded construction. The name Betty can be seen above the driver's visor and the WD Number T255310 is just visible on the hull front. Although the official caption identifies the unit as 1st RTR it does not appear on the list shown on page 6.

Photographed in the town of Stadtlohn in western Germany on 31 March 1944, this Cromwell Mk IV of 5th Royal Inniskilling Dragoon Guards is unmarked except for the WD Number T188397. Note the commander's ARV cupola and the fencing wire holding the foliage camouflage in place.

Notes

1. In addition to the armoured reconnaissance regiment the divisional headquarters had a number of Cromwell and Centaur OP tanks on hand.

29th Armoured Brigade. Attached to 11th Armoured Division in June 1944, the brigade was made up of 23rd Hussars, 3rd Royal Tank Regiment and 2nd Fife and Forfar Yeomanry. The brigade took part in the fighting in Normandy and the advance through Belgium and Holland with the three tank regiments equipped throughout with American Sherman tanks (1).

By December 1944 the brigade had been withdrawn from the front to be equipped with the new Comet Cruisers, armed with the 77mm High Velocity (HV) gun, and Cromwell CS tanks.

The brigade's conversion to the Comet was interrupted by the German Ardennes Offensive when the regiments were briefly returned to the front line in their old Shermans and the new tanks were involved in limited operations only before the war ended.

6th Airborne Reconnaissance Regiment. Originally formed as a single squadron in July 1941 by the time of the Normandy landings this formation had been expanded to a full regiment and attached to 6th Airborne Division. Initially equipped with Tetrach light tanks, on Tuesday, 1 August 1944 a party of two officers and forty-three other ranks

were detached from the regiment to receive training on the Cromwell tank and by the following Sunday the trainees had returned with eight tanks. These were allocated to A Squadron under Major Paul Barnett, a Royal Tank Regiment officer, and organised into two troops. By the end of the month a further four Cromwells arrived and these were formed into a third troop.

The regiment took part in Operation Paddle, the advance to the Seine, reporting the loss of just one Cromwell in the fighting to take the town of Pont L'Eveque on Tuesday, 22 August 1944. On the following Saturday, in the regiment's last action in Normandy, a Cromwell commanded by Sergeant Thompson of 1 Troop, although badly damaged, destroyed a German anti-tank position enabling the paratroopers to occupy Pont Audemer an important road junction on the river Risle, the last natural obstacle before the Seine.

During the first week of September the regiment was withdrawn from France.

Although attached to the airborne division it should be noted that the Tetrach and Cromwell crews were assembled from RAC units.

Although the official caption to this image states that the Cromwell Mk IV seen here is from 2nd Northamptonshire Yeomanry, the arm of service sign of a white 40 on a black square, to the left of the driver's visor, identifies the unit as the headquarters of 11th Armoured Division. The famous Black Bull formation badge is clearly visible to the right of the hull machine gun below the name Oliver. Note that both tanks have motorcycles strapped to the side of their turrets.

Photographed in the town of Dongen in Holland on 1 November 1944 during the fighting along the river Maas this Cromwell Mk IV of B Squadron, 8th King's Royal Irish Hussars is based on a Type F hull, the final variant. Note that the WD Number T188206 has been repeated on the turret side below the squadron sign. The A30 Challenger in the background is one of a number passed on to the Hussars from 22nd Armoured Brigade in August when these vehicles were replaced by Fireflies in the tank squadrons.

ARMOURED RECONNAISSANCE REGIMENT, JUNE 1944

The armoured reconnaissance regiments of the armoured divisions were organised similarly to the tank regiments without the added 'punch' of the Fireflies and the formation shown here is based on War Establishment (WE) II/151/3 of 30 November 1943. As the campaign progressed the reconnaissance units were increasingly employed as an extra tank regiment and their intended role was undertaken by the armoured car regiments.

REGIMENTAL HEADQUARTERS

Cromwell 75mm   Cromwell 75mm   Cromwell 75mm   Cromwell 75mm

Headquarters Squadron

Admin Troop

The regimental Admin Troop was arranged similarly to that of the squadrons.

Anti-aircraft Troop

6 x Crusader AA tanks

Recce Troop

11 x Stuart light tanks

Link Troop

9 x Scout cars

A Squadron 45 △   **B Squadron** 45 ☐   **C Squadron** 45 ○

      As for A Squadron   As for A Squadron

Squadron Headquarters

Cromwell 75mm   Cromwell 75mm   Cromwell 95mm   Cromwell 95mm   Cromwell ARV

1 Troop   **2 Troop**   **3 Troop**   **4 Troop**   **5 Troop**

                 As for 1 Troop   As for 1 Troop   As for 1 Troop   As for 1 Troop

Cromwell 75mm   Cromwell 75mm   Cromwell 75mm

Each squadron headquarters also contained an Admin Troop equipped with a number of lorries, halftracks, carriers and a kitchen van.

Notes

1. The reconnaissance troops of the tank regiments of 22 Armoured Brigade also received a number of these tanks which were intended to replace the Stuart.

2. 20th Armoured Brigade was an independent formation until its disbandment in April 1943.

8th King's Royal Irish Hussars. As with many of the units of 7th Armoured Division, this regiment had served in North Africa and the Mediterranean returning to England in late 1943 to re-equip and train as the division's armoured reconnaissance regiment.

Commanded by Lieutenant-Colonel Cuthbert Goulburn, the regiment took part in all the division's major engagements including the disastrous action at Villers-Bocage in July 1944. The regiment was involved in the fighting around Mont Pincon and at the crossing of the Dives in late August acting, in fact, as a fourth tank regiment.

In November the Hussars were withdrawn from the front line as so many men were due for repatriation to Britain having accumulated four years overseas service.

The regiment returned in January 1945 taking part in the battles in the Roer and in March led the division in Operation Varsity, the crossing of the Rhine. In April 1945 a number of the regiment's Cromwells were replaced by M24 light tanks (1) and during this time the Hussars fought their way into Germany liberating over 20,000 Allied prisoners at Fallingbostel, east of Bremen.

In the last days of the war, together with the men of 1st Battalion, The Rifle Brigade, the regiment was the first Allied unit to enter Hamburg.

From 1941, when the regiment had first been issued with American Stuart light tanks, until their service in the Korean conflict the 8th Hussars named their tanks after famous horses for the regimental headquarters and A and C squadrons. The tanks of B Squadron were named for foxhounds. The names all began with the squadron letter while the headquarters used the letter H, Lieutenant-Colonel Goulburn's tank being name 'Hurry On'.

2nd Northamptonshire Yeomanry. In 1943 this unit, which had been part of 20th Armoured Brigade, was converted to an armoured reconnaissance regiment and attached to 11th Armoured Division (2).

The regiment landed in Normandy in June 1944 and as it was usually in the vanguard of the division's operations suffered heavily, particularly in the battles along the Odon and in the fighting for Carpiquet airfield in late June 1944 where a complete squadron of tanks was lost in a single day.

In early July, following the Epsom and Goodwood battles, the regiment was formed into a battlegroup with 8th Battalion The Rifle Brigade and this

....text continued on page 13

Photographed near Bremen on 12 April 1945, the Cromwell and Challenger seen here are both from 8th King's Royal Irish Hussars. Although it is difficult to be certain, this tank is probably a Mk V with the large outward-opening driver's hatch installed in some vehicles built by Vauxhall. Note the traces of what appears to be disruptive camouflage on the turret front and sides. The name Abbot's Pride II is just visible on the side of the turret suggesting that this is an A Squadron tank.

Tanks of the 8th King's Royal Irish Hussars, at least some from A Squadron, formed up in preparation for the advance into Germany on 29 March 1945. The combined unit serial and 7th Armoured Division formation sign, illustrated on page 21, are clearly visible on each vehicle. Note the large white recognition star on the turret roof of the Mk VI in the foreground and the disruptive camouflage on the Challengers in the background.

Photographed in the town of Flers, south-west of Falaise, this Cromwell Mk IV is from 2nd Northamptonshire Yeomanry identified by the 11th Armoured Division formation badge and the arm of service sign of a white number 45 on a green over blue square. Note the Bren gun on the turret roof and that the tank's WD Number, T187827, is repeated on the turret side. The significance of the names Marie and Jean is uncertain but many accounts mention French girls writing or painting their names and telephone numbers on the sides of Allied vehicles.

This Cromwell Mk IV tank of 2nd Northamptonshire Yeomanry, photographed in Vassy, a small town on the Vire to Falaise road, may be from the regimental headquarters. The arm of service sign of a white number 45 on a green over blue square can be seen to the left of the driver's position and the lack of contrast between the two colours in monochrome images is obvious. Given the location and the official date of 5 August, this photograph must have been taken shortly before the regiment was disbanded.

A sergeant of the Royal Electrical and Mechanical Engineers at work on a Cromwell tank of C Squadron, 2nd Northamptonshire Yeomanry. This image provides a good view of at least one type of the rubber strips that were applied to this squadron's tanks at some time in August 1944. The markings of C Squadron's Cromwell tanks are discussed further on page 22 of the Camouflage and Markings section of this book.

....text continued from page 10

arrangement would last until August when, at a fraction of its original strength, the 2nd Northamptonshire Yeomanry was disbanded.

Interestingly the regiment is said to have had three Fireflies on hand during the fighting in Normandy.

15th/19th The King's Royal Hussars.

The regiment served as part of the British Expeditionary Force (BEF) in France in 1940 after which it remained in the United Kingdom until August 1944 when it was sent to Normandy to replace 2nd Northamptonshire Yeomanry as the armoured reconnaissance regiment of 11th Armoured Division.

In September the regiment was detached from 11th Armoured Division to support XXX Corps in its advance across the Escaut Canal at Lille-St-Hubert as part of Operation Market Garden. By November the regiment had returned to its parent formation and took part in the fighting along the River Maas in Holland.

In March 1945 the regiment was re-equipped with Comet tanks retaining some of their Cromwell CS tanks and a number of Challengers.

With 11th Armoured Division the Hussars advanced into Germany reaching the Baltic coast between Lubeck and Hamburg when the war ended. The regiment's tanks were named, beginning with the squadron letter, and known examples suggest the names were chosen from classical mythology. Photographic evidence indicates that most names were covered or removed after the Normandy battles.

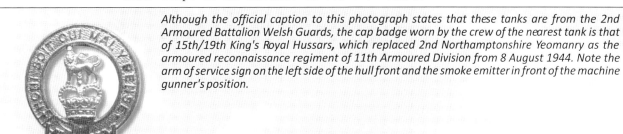

Although the official caption to this photograph states that these tanks are from the 2nd Armoured Battalion Welsh Guards, the cap badge worn by the crew of the nearest tank is that of 15th/19th King's Royal Hussars, which replaced 2nd Northamptonshire Yeomanry as the armoured reconnaissance regiment of 11th Armoured Division from 8 August 1944. Note the arm of service sign on the left side of the hull front and the smoke emitter in front of the machine gunner's position.

Notes

1. The title of this battalion differs in several accounts and I have chosen the name used in *The Story of the Guards Armoured Division* by Captain Laurence M. Harvey, the Earl of Rosse and Lieutenant-Colonel Edward R. Hill DSO, both of who served with the division during the war.

2nd Armoured Reconnaissance Battalion Welsh Guards. As the armoured reconnaissance regiment of the Guards Armoured Division this unit went into action for the first time on 18 June 1944 between Cagny and Le Poirier in Normandy near the Orne river (1).

In late August, with the German retreat, the battalion was sent into Belgium as part of what became known as 'The Great Swan', advancing towards Brussels. From 1 September 1944 the battalion was paired with 1st Battalion Welsh Guards and this arrangement, referred to within the division as the Welsh Group, was maintained until the end of the war.

On 3 September, after an unsuccessful attempt by elements of the Household Cavalry Regiment and a battalion of the Grenadier Guards to capture the city, the Cromwell of Lieutenant Dent of 1 Squadron, Welsh Guards entered Brussels, the first Allied tank to do so.

The battalion took part in Operation Market Garden and in the subsequent fighting in Holland which continued into the winter.

On 30 March 1945 the battalion crossed the Rhine, capturing Oldenzaal without a fight and pressing on into Germany. During much of this time the battalion was split into individual squadrons and allocated to whichever infantry formation required armoured support.

By 18 April the tanks of the Welsh Guards had reached Visselhövede, south of Bremen, were the headquarters units found themselves surrounded by a German naval infantry formation and were forced to fight their way out with the help of the tanks of 1 Squadron. On 26 April 1945 the Welsh Guards captured the SS barracks at Westertimke, approximately 20 kilometres north-east of Bremen and this was to be their last action of the war.

In keeping with their traditions as infantry formations, the Guards armoured squadrons were numbered and not referred to by letters.

A Cromwell Mk IV of No. 2 Squadron, 2nd Armoured Battalion Welsh Guards, photographed near Escoville on 18 July 1944, the first day of Operation Goodwood. The lower hull displays a full set of markings including, from left to right, the arm of service sign of an armoured reconnaissance regiment, a bridging classification marking, a squadron sign enclosing the troop number and the formation badge of the Guards Armoured Division. The markings of these tanks are also shown and discussed on pages 18 and 21 of the Camouflage and Markings section.

Photographed during what was perhaps the Guards' most celebrated action of the North-West Europe campaign, Operation Market Garden, a number of Cromwell tanks of 2nd Armoured Battalion Welsh Guards is shown crossing the bridge at Nijmegen on 21 September 1944. A large No. 1 Squadron sign, enclosing a troop number 4, is just visible on the left rear hull of the nearest tank. Note also the exhaust cowl and the large ammunition box fitted to the turret rear and marked with a white star.

During the fighting in Belgium this Cromwell IV of Number 3 Squadron, 2nd Armoured Battalion Welsh Guards was used to ferry wounded German prisoners to an aid post. Note the squadron sign on the hull locker in white identifying an un-brigaded regiment, the turret stowage box and the Bren gun in front of the commander's hatch. Note also the very basic array of markings compared to the tanks photographed earlier in the campaign and shown on page 14.

Also photographed during Operation Market Garden, this Cromwell tank, possibly a Mk VI, of No.3 Squadron, 2nd Armoured Battalion, is travelling along the road to Nijmegen which came to be known as Hell's Highway. The large squadron sign, in the white of an un-brigaded regiment, is clearly visible on the hull rear and has been repeated on the stowage locker on the side of the vehicle.

Photographed outside Westertimke, near Bremen in western Germany, where the Guards fought their last action of the war, these three tanks were all disabled by hand-held anti-tank weapons. The markings are typical of No. 1 Squadron, 2nd Welsh Guards and include the large squadron sign in white with a dark centre enclosing the troop number. The addition of ammunition boxes along the hull sides and at the turret rear was a common field modification.

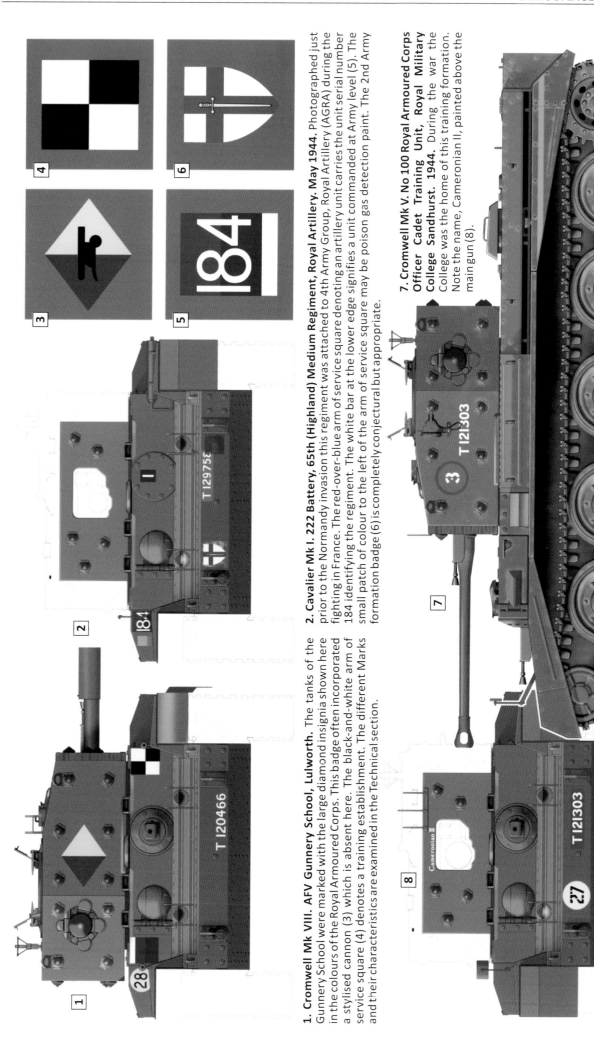

1. Cromwell Mk VIII. AFV Gunnery School, Lulworth. The tanks of the Gunnery School were marked with the large diamond insignia shown here in the colours of the Royal Armoured Corps. This badge often incorporated a stylised cannon (3) which is absent here. The black-and-white arm of service square (4) denotes a training establishment. The different Marks and their characteristics are examined in the Technical section.

2. Cavalier Mk I. 222 Battery, 65th (Highland) Medium Regiment, Royal Artillery. May 1944. Photographed just prior to the Normandy invasion this regiment was attached to 4th Army Group, Royal Artillery (AGRA) during the fighting in France. The red-over-blue arm of service square denoting an artillery unit carries the unit serial number 184 identifying the regiment. The white bar at the lower edge signifies a unit commanded at Army level (5). The small patch of colour to the left of the arm of service square may be poison gas detection paint. The 2nd Army formation badge (6) is completely conjectural but appropriate.

7. Cromwell Mk V. No 100 Royal Armoured Corps Officer Cadet Training Unit, Royal Military College Sandhurst. 1944. During the war the College was the home of this training formation. Note the name, Cameronian II, painted above the main gun (8).

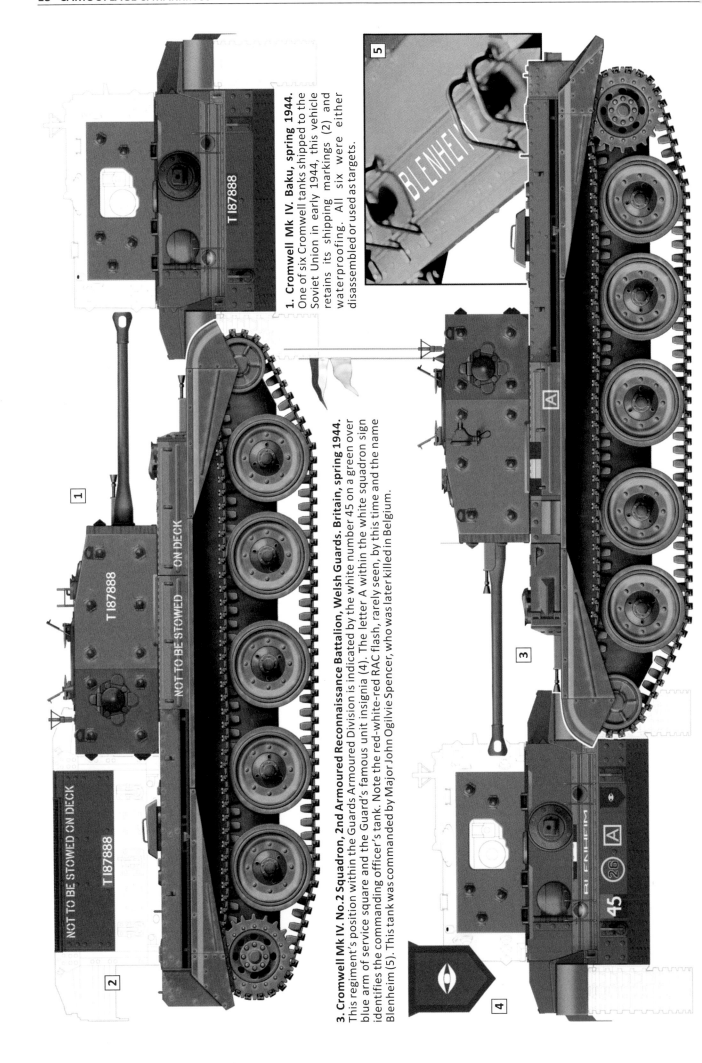

1. Cromwell Mk IV. Baku, spring 1944.
One of six Cromwell tanks shipped to the Soviet Union in early 1944, this vehicle retains its shipping markings (2) and waterproofing. All six were either disassembled or used as targets.

3. Cromwell Mk IV. No.2 Squadron, 2nd Armoured Reconnaissance Battalion, Welsh Guards. Britain, spring 1944.
This regiment's position within the Guards Armoured Division is indicated by the white number 45 on a green over blue arm of service square and the Guard's famous unit insignia (4). The letter A within the white squadron sign identifies the commanding officer's tank. Note the red-white-red RAC flash, rarely seen, by this time and the name Blenheim (5). This tank was commanded by Major John Ogilvie Spencer, who was later killed in Belgium.

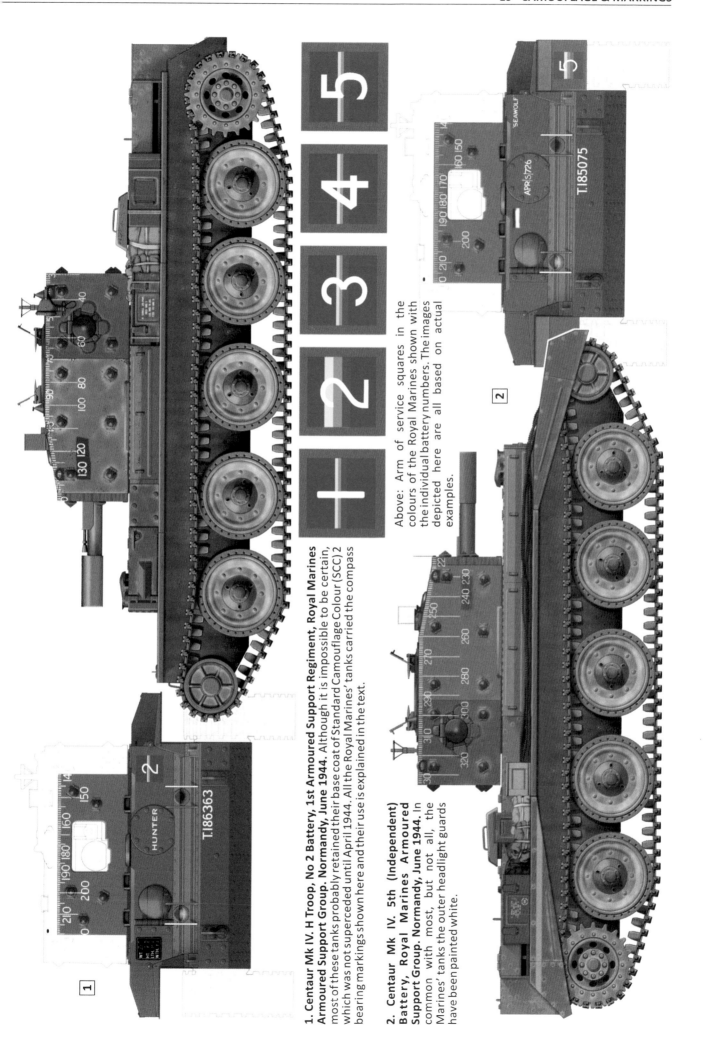

1. Centaur Mk IV. H Troop, No 2 Battery, 1st Armoured Support Regiment, Royal Marines Armoured Support Group. Normandy, June 1944. Although it is impossible to be certain, most of these tanks probably retained their base coat of Standard Camouflage Colour (SCC) 2 which was not superceded until April 1944. All the Royal Marines' tanks carried the compass bearing markings shown here and their use is explained in the text.

2. Centaur Mk IV. 5th (Independent) Battery, Royal Marines Armoured Support Group. Normandy, June 1944. In common with most, but not all, the Marines' tanks the outer headlight guards have been painted white.

Above: Arm of service squares in the colours of the Royal Marines shown with the individual battery numbers. The images depicted here are all based on actual examples.

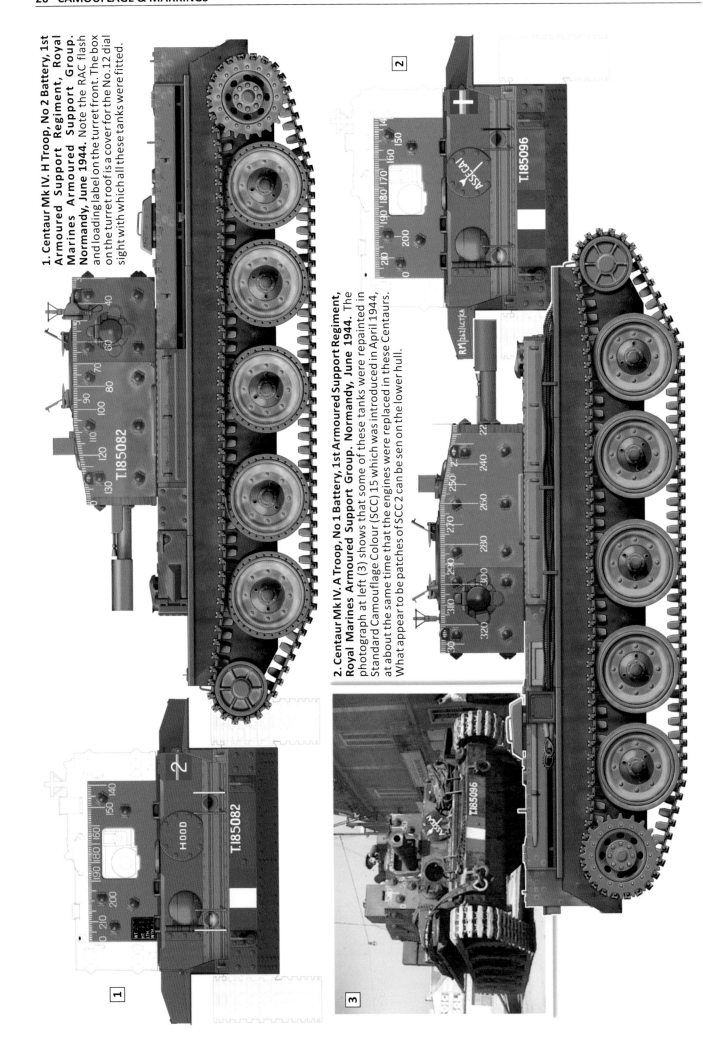

1. Centaur Mk IV. H Troop, No 2 Battery, 1st Armoured Support Regiment, Royal Marines Armoured Support Group. Normandy, June 1944. Note the RAC flash and loading label on the turret front. The box on the turret roof is a cover for the No.12 dial sight with which all these tanks were fitted.

2. Centaur Mk IV. A Troop, No 1 Battery, 1st Armoured Support Regiment, Royal Marines Armoured Support Group. Normandy, June 1944. The photograph at left (3) shows that some of these tanks were repainted in Standard Camouflage Colour (SCC) 15 which was introduced in April 1944, at about the same time that the engines were replaced in these Centaurs. What appear to be patches of SCC 2 can be seen on the lower hull.

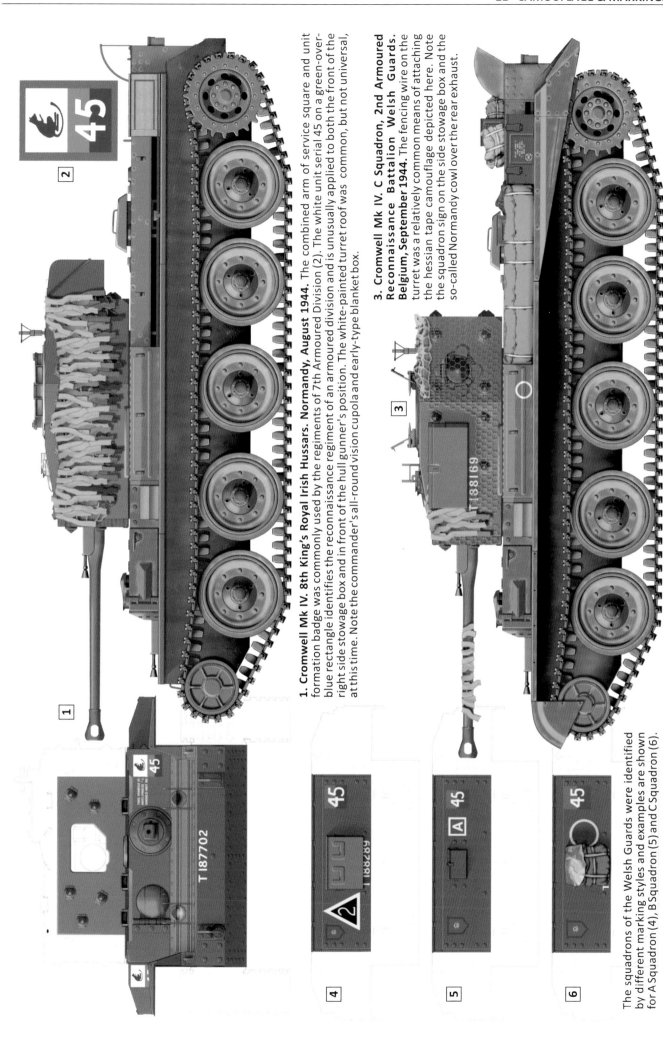

1. Cromwell Mk IV. 8th King's Royal Irish Hussars. Normandy, August 1944. The combined arm of service square and unit formation badge was commonly used by the regiments of 7th Armoured Division (2). The white unit serial 45 on a green-over-blue rectangle identifies the reconnaissance regiment of an armoured division and is unusually applied to both the front of the right side stowage box and in front of the hull gunner's position. The white-painted turret roof was common, but not universal, at this time. Note the commander's all-round vision cupola and early-type blanket box.

3. Cromwell Mk IV. C Squadron, 2nd Armoured Reconnaissance Battalion Welsh Guards. Belgium, September 1944. The fencing wire on the turret was a relatively common means of attaching the hessian tape camouflage depicted here. Note the squadron sign on the side stowage box and the so-called Normandy cowl over the rear exhaust.

The squadrons of the Welsh Guards were identified by different marking styles and examples are shown for A Squadron (4), B Squadron (5) and C Squadron (6).

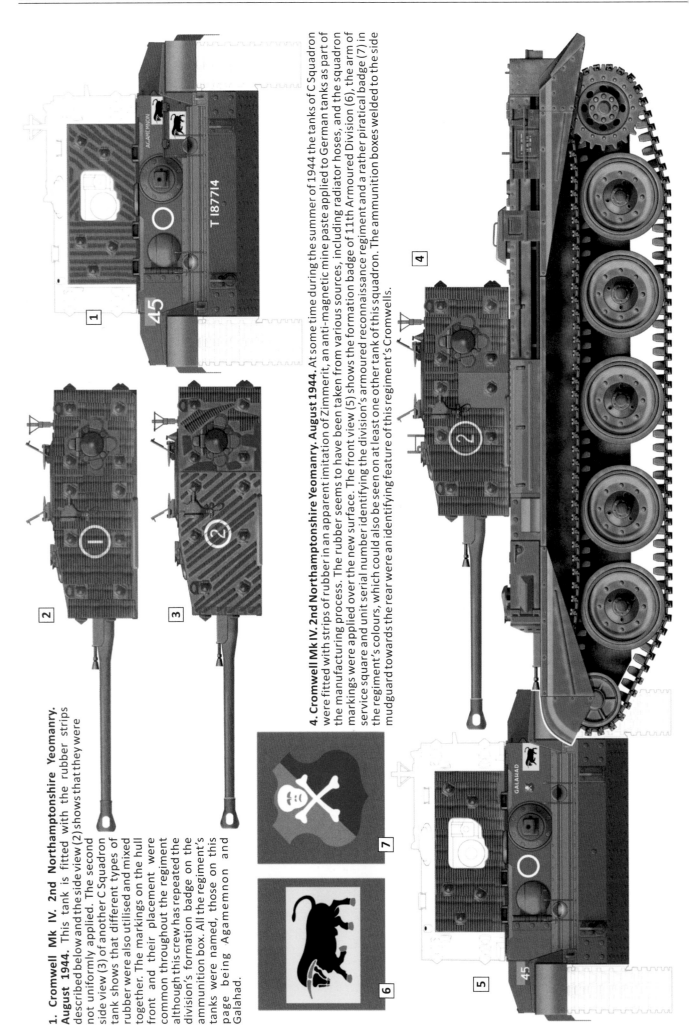

1. Cromwell Mk IV. 2nd Northamptonshire Yeomanry. August 1944. This tank is fitted with the rubber strips described below and the side view (2) shows that they were not uniformly applied. The second side view (3) of another C Squadron tank shows that different types of rubber were also utilised and mixed together. The markings on the hull front and their placement were common throughout the regiment although this crew has repeated the division's formation badge on the ammunition box. All the regiment's tanks were named, those on this page being Agamemnon and Galahad.

4. Cromwell Mk IV. 2nd Northamptonshire Yeomanry. August 1944. At some time during the summer of 1944 the tanks of C Squadron were fitted with strips of rubber in an apparent imitation of Zimmerit, an anti-magnetic mine paste applied to German tanks as part of the manufacturing process. The rubber seems to have been taken from various sources, including radiator hoses, and the squadron markings were applied over the new surface. The front view (5) shows the formation badge of 11th Armoured Division (6), the arm of service square and unit serial number identifying the division's armoured reconnaissance regiment and a rather piratical badge (7) in the regiment's colours, which could also be seen on at least one other tank of this squadron. The ammunition boxes welded to the side mudguard towards the rear were an identifying feature of this regiment's Cromwells.

1. Cromwell Mk IV Type F. 13th Royal Horse Artillery (Honourable Artillery Company), 11th Armoured Division. Germany, early 1945. Commanded by Lieutenant Colonel R. B. T. Daniell, this AOP tank carries the white unit serial number 76 on a red-over-

-blue square denoting the second senior artillery regiment of a division and the well-known formation badge of 11th Armoured Division. The small tactical sign on the hull front (2) identifies the commanding officer of an artillery regiment. Note that the main gun, although convincing, is a dummy.

3. Cromwell IV. M Battery, 3rd Royal Horse Artillery, 7th Armoured Division. Germany, March 1945. Displayed on the hull front are the combined 7th Armoured Division formation badge with the 74 unit serial number identifying the division's senior artillery regiment (4). The white X of the Royal Artillery tactical sign denotes the commander of a battery.

6. Cromwell Mk IVF. 5th Royal Horse Artillery. 7th Armoured Division. Germany, April 1945. This tank displays a variation of the combined formation badge and arm of service square commonly seen on the division's vehicles. The Tactical sign made up of a white letter Z on a red-over-blue square (7) identifies the regiment's commanding officer. Also shown as an example is the tactical sign denoting the commanding officer of D Troop, 2nd Battery (8).

The turret still has the white-painted roof (9) commonly seen in Normandy and has been fitted with a .30-calibre machine gun. Note the support for the dummy gun.

Note the name PEGASUS V which has been painted on to the front of the turret. Although not shown here the tank's WD Number, T188464, was carried on the turret sides.

The batteries of the Royal Horse Artillery were referred to by letters (5) and these were usually incorporated into the tactical signs. Note that the letter on the hull front has a dark, possibly black, background.

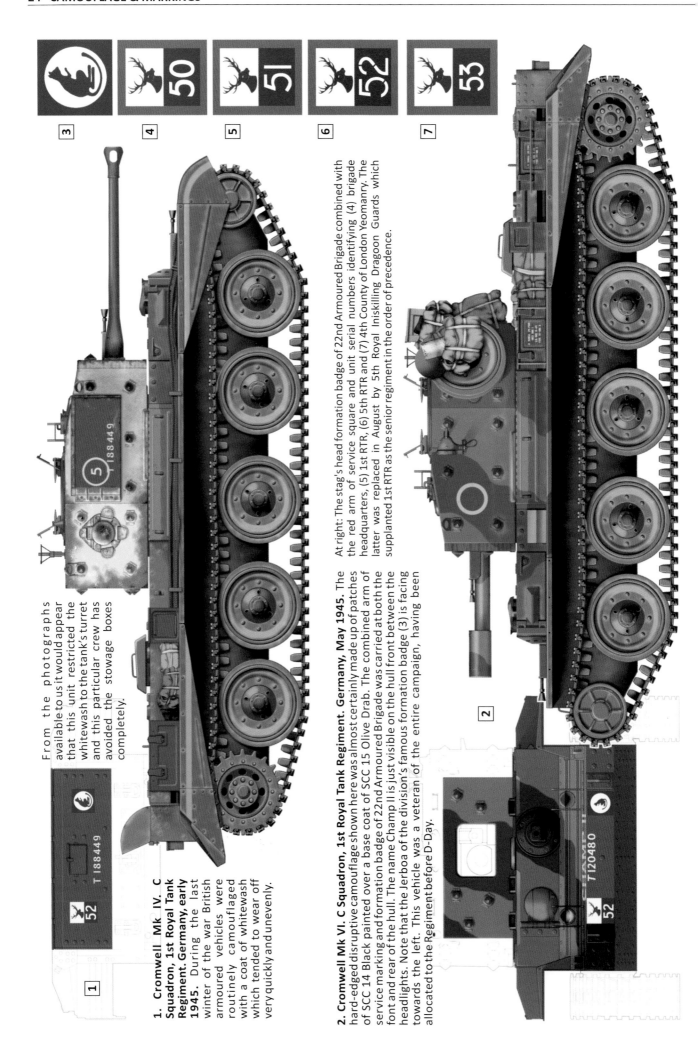

3

4 🦌 50

5 🦌 51

6 🦌 52

7 🦌 53

1

⚡ 52 🦏

T 188449

From the photographs available to us it would appear that this unit restricted the whitewash to the tank's turret and this particular crew has avoided the stowage boxes completely.

1. Cromwell Mk IV. C Squadron, 1st Royal Tank Regiment. Germany, early 1945. During the last winter of the war British armoured vehicles were routinely camouflaged with a coat of whitewash which tended to wear off very quickly and unevenly.

2. Cromwell Mk VI. C Squadron, 1st Royal Tank Regiment. Germany, May 1945. The hard-edged disruptive camouflage shown here was almost certainly made up of patches of SCC 14 Black painted over a base coat of SCC 15 Olive Drab. The combined arm of service marking and formation badge of 22nd Armoured Brigade was carried at both the front and rear of the hull. The name Champ II is just visible on the hull front between the headlights. Note that the Jerboa of the division's famous formation badge (3) is facing towards the left. This vehicle was a veteran of the entire campaign, having been allocated to the Regiment before D-Day.

At right: The stag's head formation badge of 22nd Armoured Brigade combined with the red arm of service square and unit serial numbers identifying (4) brigade headquarters, (5) 1st RTR, (6) 5th RTR and (7) 4th County of London Yeomanry. The latter was replaced in August by 5th Royal Iniskilling Dragoon Guards which supplanted 1st RTR as the senior regiment in the order of precedence.

2

⚡ 52 T 120480 🦏

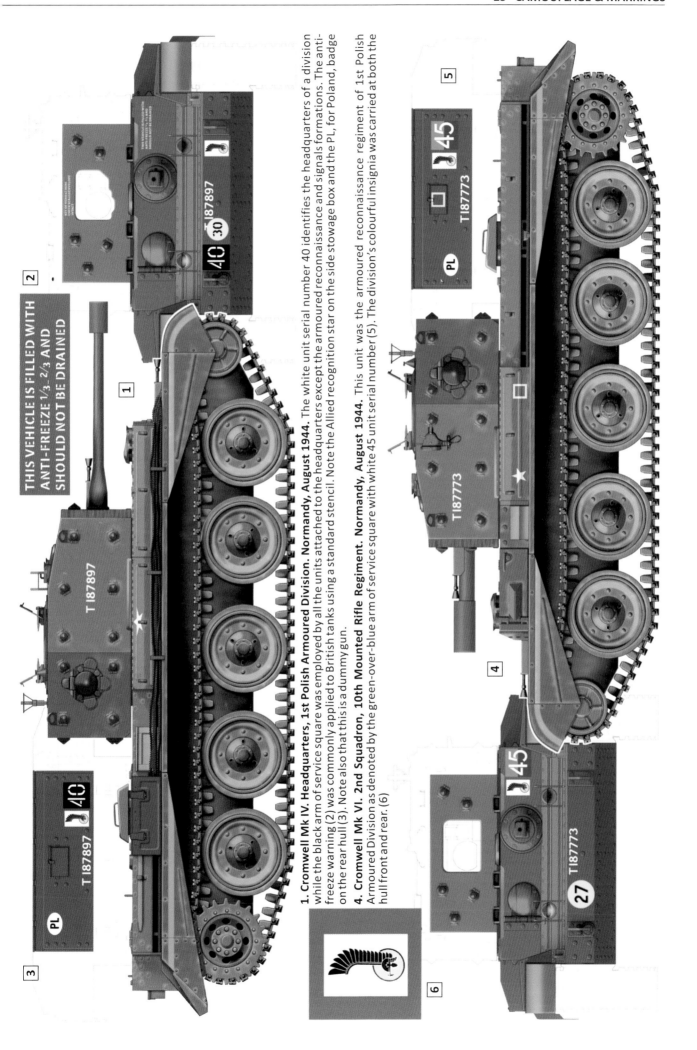

1. Cromwell Mk IV. Headquarters, 1st Polish Armoured Division. Normandy, August 1944. The white unit serial number 40 identifies the headquarters of a division while the black arm of service square was employed by all the units attached to the headquarters except the armoured reconnaissance and signals formations. The anti-freeze warning (2) was commonly applied to British tanks using a standard stencil. Note the Allied recognition star on the side stowage box and the PL, for Poland, badge on the rear hull (3). Note also that this is a dummy gun.

4. Cromwell Mk VI. 2nd Squadron, 10th Mounted Rifle Regiment. Normandy, August 1944. This unit was the armoured reconnaissance regiment of 1st Polish Armoured Division as denoted by the green-over-blue arm of service square with white 45 unit serial number (5). The division's colourful insignia was carried at both the hull front and rear. (6)

THIS VEHICLE IS FILLED WITH ANTI-FREEZE ⅓ – ⅔ AND SHOULD NOT BE DRAINED

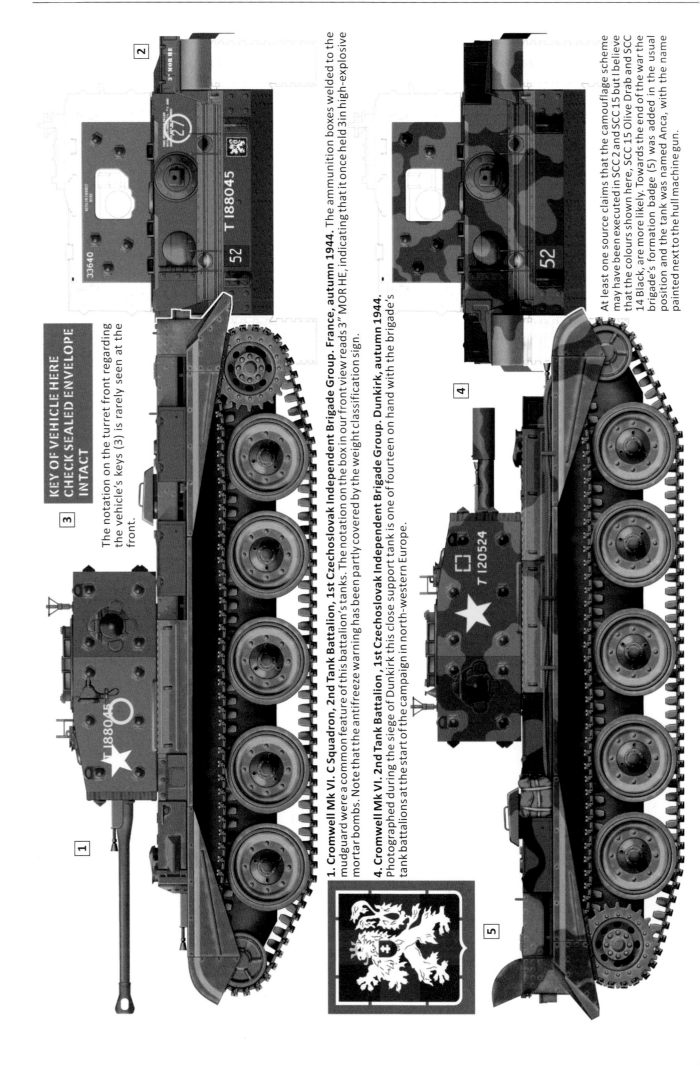

KEY OF VEHICLE HERE
CHECK SEALED ENVELOPE
INTACT

The notation on the turret front regarding the vehicle's keys (3) is rarely seen at the front.

1. Cromwell Mk VI. C Squadron, 2nd Tank Battalion, 1st Czechoslovak Independent Brigade Group. France, autumn 1944. The ammunition boxes welded to the mudguard were a common feature of this battalion's tanks. The notation on the box in our front view reads 3" MOR HE, indicating that it once held 3in high-explosive mortar bombs. Note that the antifreeze warning has been partly covered by the weight classification sign.

4. Cromwell Mk VI. 2nd Tank Battalion, 1st Czechoslovak Independent Brigade Group. Dunkirk, autumn 1944. Photographed during the siege of Dunkirk this close support tank is one of fourteen on hand with the brigade's tank battalions at the start of the campaign in north-western Europe.

At least one source claims that the camouflage scheme may have been executed in SCC 2 and SCC 15 but I believe that the colours shown here, SCC 15 Olive Drab and SCC 14 Black, are more likely. Towards the end of the war the brigade's formation badge (5) was added in the usual position and the tank was named Anca, with the name painted next to the hull machine gun.

CENTAUR
CS Mk IV
1ST ROYAL MARINE
ARMOURED SUPPORT
REGIMENT

NORMANDY, JUNE 1944
1/35 SCALE
MARCOS SERRA

The finished Tamiya 1/35 scale model, less the tracks, primed and ready for the first coat of paint. Below: After a coat of Future gloss the kit decals were applied including the loading information, next to the driver's hatch, name and arm of service marking.

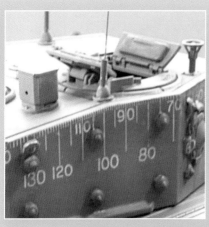

The completed model with a replica of a Royal Marines Sherman V which Marcos built at the same time as the Centaur. The Sherman was featured in detail in the second book in the TankCraft series, Sherman Tank: British Army and Royal Marines, Normandy Campaign 1944.

CROMWELL Mk IV
B SQUADRON 2ND BATTALION WELSH GUARDS
NORMANDY, JUNE 1944
1/35 SCALE
TAN ZHIYONG

Based on the 1/35 scale Tamiya Cromwell Mk IV kit this model also has a number of added details including the turret stowage boxes, the fuel can rack on the mudguard towards the rear and the vane sight in front of the commander's cupola.

The system of markings used by this regiment is examined in the Camouflage and Markings section of this book on page 21.

Small details to note are the electrical lead for the turret spotlight, straps and clasps for the tools and the locks of the stowage boxes. Note also how the white Allied recognition star covers part of the ventilator dome in the turret roof.

CENTAUR Mk IV
LEYLAND MANUFACTURED
ENGLAND, LATE 1943

1/35 SCALE
SHENG HUI

Note the very subtle weathering of the wheels, tracks and lower hull. A photograph of this model before the paint was applied can be seen on page 48.

Although at first glance this model appears to be quite unremarkable, a closer examination reveals a surprising amount of detail including the new headlight brush guards, Modelkasten tracks and photo-etched hinges and locks.

CROMWELL Mk IV
HEADQUARTERS 4TH COUNTY OF LONDON YEOMANRY

NORMANDY, JUNE 1944
1/48 SCALE
SHIN OIKAWA

Japanese modeller Shin Oikawa's 1/48 scale Tamiya build was inspired by photographs of one of the tanks lost during the battle at Villers-Bocage in July 1944. Although the markings are somewhat speculative they are nonetheless impressive as is the amount of detail incorporated into this relatively small model.

CROMWELL CS Mk IV
A SQUADRON 10TH POLISH MOUNTED RIFLE REGIMENT
HOLLAND, NOVEMBER 1944
1/35 SCALE
TOMASZ BOHDAN POROSILO

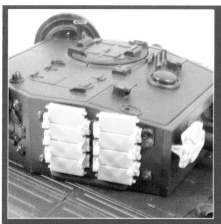

The photographs on this page show the model in various stages of completion including, at top right, the pre-shading which gives the finished product such a realistic look. Tomasz used tracks from three different manufacturers in plastic and metal. The turret and hull, however, were built almost straight from the box although the mudguards and fenders were dramatically thinned. The markings of the 1st Polish Armoured Division are examined in the Camouflage and Markings section on page 25.

Front and rear views of the completed model. The weathering, although extensive, is very realistic and totally believable, avoiding effects which could easily be overdone. The damage to the mudguards is also quite convincing and notice that the markings at the hull front are accurately applied to the spare lengths of track.

Until the 1990s the only available model of the Cromwell tank was produced by Airfix in 1/32 scale. First released in 1971 the Airfix Cromwell was last advertised in the company's 1980 catalogue and was essentially a toy, made in a semi-rigid plastic with minimal, and often inaccurate, detail. In 1990 Accurate Armour released a resin model of the Cromwell VII/VIII and this was soon superseded by a multi-media kit which included resin, photo-etched brass and white metal parts.

Although of the highest quality, short-run production models such as the Accurate Armour Cromwell can be prohibitively expensive and it was not until 1997 that modellers of British armour were rewarded for their patience with the release of Tamiya's 1/35 scale Cromwell IV, a highly detailed

and accurate injection-moulded kit, which was soon followed by the Centaur CS version.

In 2001 Revell released a 1/72 model of the Cromwell IV which set a new standard in accuracy and detail in this scale. Several companies produce extra detail and conversion sets for the Revell model. Although unavailable for some time it was re-released in 2012. Almost ironically, one of the latest releases is the Airfix kit in the company's other favourite scale of 1/76. As with the first books in this series I have chosen to concentrate on the most popular modelling scale of 1/35, although I have tried to include a selection of items from some of the smaller scale producers. A list of manufacturers, together with suggestions for further reading, can be found on page 64 of this book.

TAMIYA

This Japanese company has transformed itself from a post-war sawmill, which sold wooden models as a sideline, into the largest producer of scale model kits in the world.

First released in 1997 to rave reviews, Tamiya's 1/35 scale Cromwell is still the most easily accessible model of this tank. Optional parts are

included for the Normandy exhaust cowl and the Culin hedgerow-cutting device in addition to a number of photo-etched brass pieces. The 1/48 scale Cromwell Mk IV is a relatively new release and is obviously based on the larger kit. The 1/35 scale Centaur model utilises most of the Cromwell kit with a new turret and 95mm gun.

  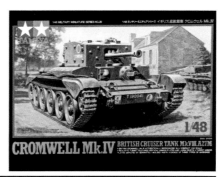

Above, from left to right: Tamiya's currently available Cromwell and Centaur kits. At right: The 1/35 scale Centaur CS Mk IV model built as a Cromwell with, inset, the Centaur model in the markings of the Royal Marine Armoured Support Group.

Below: The Tamiya 1/48 scale Cromwell Mk IV. At left: The Tamiya 1/48 scale kit built with added details from Eduard Model Accessories. This kit is essentially a scaled-down version of the company's 1/35 scale offering.

AIRFIX

Many thousands of modellers were first introduced to the hobby through Airfix and today the brand is viewed as something of an institution. Few model companies can claim to have been the subject of a television documentary which extolled the educational, social and intellectual benefits of assembling its models. As mentioned earlier, Airfix offered a soft-plastic 1/32 scale model of the Cromwell in 1971 which is still sought by collectors today. It was never intended to be an accurate replica and was in fact one offering from a complete range which included fortifications and miniature figures. It should be remembered that at that time 1/32 scale was a popular figure size, complimenting as it did the aircraft kits of many manufacturers. The 1/76 scale Cromwell IV was released in 2011, after the company's takeover by Hornby, and is a completely new kit. For ease of assembly the tracks are cast in one piece and two very welcome inclusions are the optional hedgerow cutter and the deep wading gear, although it is almost certain that the former was never fitted in combat.

Below: The Airfix 1/76 scale Cromwell assembled with the deep wading stacks. At right: The single-piece tracks mentioned above.

REVELL

This American company's history dates back to 1943 and, like Airfix in Britain, Revell has gone through a number of changes of ownership. In 1986 the company was merged with Monogram, another famous name, and at about the same time Revell Plastics, the company's German subsidiary, began production of a range of highly-detailed 1/72 scale military vehicles. First released in 2001, the 1/72 scale Cromwell kit contains 127 detailed parts, quite a large number for a small scale kit, including small tow hooks and headlights. The kit was unavailable for some time and was also marketed by the Japanese company Ace but in 2012 the Cromwell was re-released under the Revell logo with a new set of transfers. As with most Cromwell kits a Culin hedgerow cutter is included and modellers should be aware that this was only fitted to a test vehicle in England and probably never used at the front. Like the Airfix kit, conversion and update sets are produced for the Revell Crowwell by several manufacturers including Black Dog, Eduard Model Accessories, and Dan Taylor Modelworks.

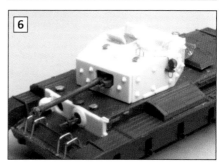

Above: 1 to 3, Details of the Revell 1/72 scale kit. 4 to 6, conversion sets produced by Black Dog, Eduard Model Accessories and Dan Taylor Modelworks.

ITALERI

This Italian company has been producing plastic models since its foundation in 1962. Of the larger model manufacturers Italeri alone has ventured into 1/56 scale, a size which complements 28mm wargames figures, and in 2014 released a kit of the Cromwell IV. Compared to the resin models available in this scale, the Italeri model is quite accurate and reasonably detailed. The kit can also serve as the basis for the conversion sets offered by S & S Models (see below).

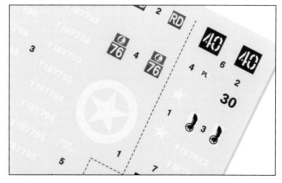

Above: The Italeri 1/56 scale Cromwell Mk IV. This kit is also marketed under the World of Tanks logo. At right: The transfer sheet from the Italeri kit and a rear view of the assembled kit.

SKP MODELS

Based in the Czech Republic, SKP Models offers complete injection-moulded kits of the Cromwell Mk IV F and Mk VI Close Support tank in 1/35 scale. The models come with photo-etched brass and resin parts and single-piece vinyl tracks. The company also produces workable Cromwell tracks in 1/35 scale and a number of transfer sheets for British and Czech vehicles.

Above, from left to right: Detail views of the SKP Models Cromwell Mk VI and the transfer sheet that accompanies the Mk IV kit. Below: The 1/35 scale Mk IV F.

ARMOURFAST

Based in the United Kingdom, this company is a subsidiary of TDL Moulding which produces the moulds for Revell, Games Workshop, EMHAR and other well-known companies. The company's range includes a number of fast-assembly armour models including a Cromwell IV in 1/72 scale. Armourfast also offer a number of accessory sets including stowage for the Cromwell and a conversion kit to build the 95mm-armed vehicle complete with the Culin hedgerow-cutting device.

MILICAST/DAN TAYLOR MODELWORKS

Based in Glasgow, this company was founded in the 1970s and since then has steadily updated and upgraded its range of resin cast models. Today Milicast offers a Battlefield Series, which caters mainly to wargamers, and a Premier Range of more detailed kits. From 2008 the company has worked closely with Dan Taylor Modelworks which deals almost exclusively with British and German subjects related to the Normandy landings in 1/76 scale. The company's founder, Dan Taylor, was a former master model maker to Milicast and Accurate Armour and the author of *Villers-Bocage Through the Lens*. Shown below are the huge landing Craft Mk 5, here complete with two Royal Marine Centaurs, with conversion sets for the Airfix (1 to 3) and Revell Cromwell (4 to 6) kits.

At left: One of three transfer sets from Dan Taylor Modelworks depicting tanks of 22nd Armoured Brigade. Other sheets cover the tanks of the Royal Marines and the Cromwells of 11th Armoured Division.

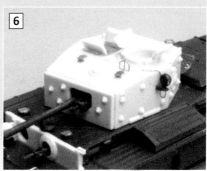

ABER

This Polish company has been manufacturing and selling upgrade sets since 1995, working in photo-etched brass, milled aluminium and brass, stainless steel and even wood. For some time now Tamiya has included a number of Aber products with their models. Shown below are details of the photo-etched brass set for the Tamiya 1/35 scale model (1 to 3) and the Tamiya 1/48 scale Cromwell kit (4 to 6). In addition ABER offer turned metal versions of the 6pdr and 75mm guns in 1/35 scale.

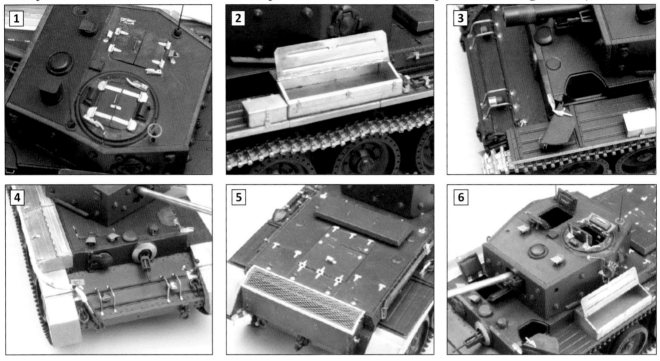

ACCURATE ARMOUR

Based in Glasgow, this company produces a line of accessory sets and complete kits with a heavy emphasis on the British and Commonwealth armies, of both the 1939-45 period and modern day. Extensive upgrade sets are available in both 1/48 and 1/35 scale. Accurate Armour also produce accessories such as a Porpoise ammunition sled, ammunition crates and transfer sets.

At left: The 1/48th scale set with deep wading trunks, waterproofed howitzer, hull machine gun and periscopes with photo-etched brass rear hull blanking plates and hull and turret trunking. Below: Tamiya's 1/48th scale Cromwell built with Accurate Armour's later stowage fittings, rotating multi-vision block cupola, split driver's hatch and Mk IV D/F deck. Inset: The 1/35th scale set designed for the Tamiya Cromwell including a complete 95mm howitzer mounting, ammunition and ammunition boxes, machine gun blanking plate, dial sight armoured cover and Porpoise sled towing points.

ARMOURSCALE

This Polish company produces a range of accessories in 1/72, 1/48 and 1/35 scale in plastic and resin of Second World War and modern period subjects. Shown here are the Cromwell burnt-out wheels (1), QF 75mm gun with machine gun (2) and British radio antenna fittings (3).

BLACK DOG

Based in the Czech Republic, this company produces a large range of detailed resin accessory and upgrade sets for armoured vehicles in 1/35, 1/48 and 1/72 scale and a number of complete kits. Shown here are stowage and camouflage sets in 1/48 scale (1 to 3) and in 1/35 scale (4 to 6).

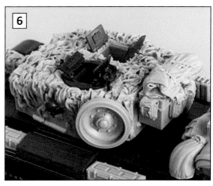

HAULER

Also based in the Czech Republic, this company produces accessory sets in photo-etched brass and resin in 1/48, 1/35 and even 1/87 scale. A number of products are also marketed under the Brengun Logo. Hauler's current catalogue contains just one upgrade set specifically aimed at the Tamiya 1/48 scale Cromwell Mk IV kit and samples are shown below.

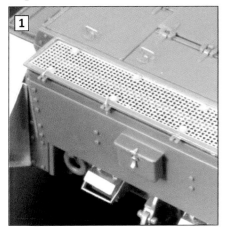

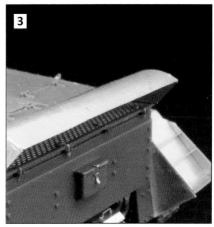

EDUARD MODEL ACCESSORIES

Founded in 1989, this Czech company produces high-quality upgrade kits in photo-etched metal and resin and a number of complete scale models all based on the US Sherman tank. Although the company manufactured a number of detail sets in 1/72, 1/48 and 1/35 scale, many of these are currently out of production although they are listed as available with some retailers.

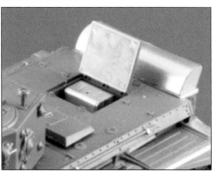

S & S MODELS

This British company produces a range of accessories and conversion kits for Italeri's 1/56th scale armoured vehicle kits. Shown here are the Italeri Cromwell built with S & S Models stowage set (1), a 95mm turret conversion set (2) and the Crowmell ARV conversion.

RB MODEL

RB Model from Poland produce a range of milled aluminium and brass gun barrels and resin accessories for 1/35 scale armour models. Shown below are, from left to right, ammunition for the 57mm OQF 6pdr gun, a highly-detailed and accurate set of British wireless antenna fittings and the muzzle brake for the 75mm ROQF Mk V gun, all in 1/35 scale.

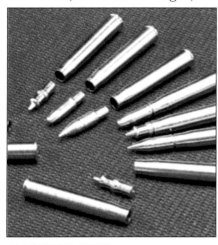 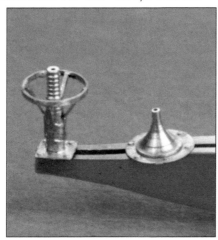 

PANZER ART

Based in Poland, this company produces an extensive range of highly-detailed accessories for Second World War and modern era armoured vehicles in resin. Show here is the Tamiya 1/35 scale Cromwell IV built with Panzer Art's stowage set with below that, the Hessian tape camouflage set (1), spare Cromwell wheels (2) and standard British fire extinguisher (3).

 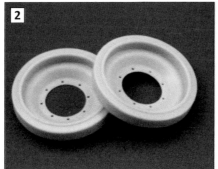 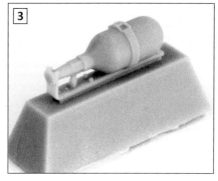

VOYAGER MODEL

Voyager have been manufacturing highly-detailed upgrade sets for scale models since 2003 with the release of their first set for 1/35 scale armour. The company produces two sets in both 1/48 scale and 1/35 scale for the Cromwell Mk IV and shown below are details of the 1/35 scale items (1-5) and the 1/48 scale detail set (6-9). Many of these parts would be appropriate for the Centaur or Mk V.

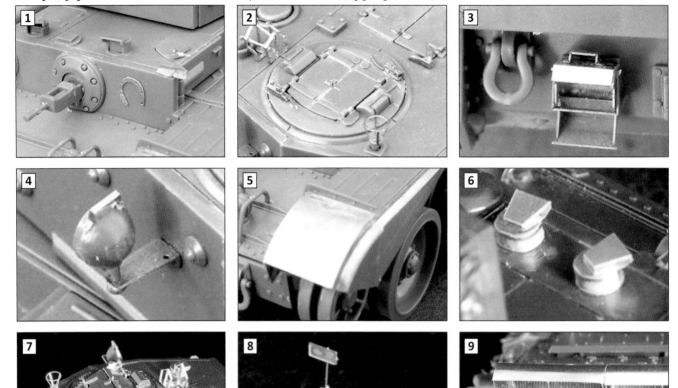

AFTERMARKET TRACKS

Although most vinyl tracks included in model kits today are reasonably detailed and accurate, many modellers still prefer to replace the standard single length of track with so-called link and length track sets or workable tracks made up, in the larger scales, of individual links. Shown below, from left to right, are track sets for the Cromwell and Centaur from Hobby Boss, Modelkasten, Spade Ace Models and Friulmodel. Eduard Model Accessories did produce a 1/72 scale set of tracks in photo-etched brass for the Revell Cromwell but my personal feeling is that these were slightly too thin and in any case the tracks that accompanied the kit were perfectly serviceable.

Below: Tamiya's Centaur Mk IV kit completed with plastic tracks from Modelkasten by Chinese modeller Sheng Hui. At left: Single-link tracks in plastic by Hobby Boss and metal Cromwell tracks by Friulmodel. At right: 1/35 scale metal track links from Spade Ace Models.

3rd Regiment Royal Horse Artillery.
Formed in 1938, the regiment was attached to 7th Armoured Division as an anti-tank formation until 1942 when it was converted to a field artillery unit.

By June 1944 the regiment was made up of D, J and M Batteries. Each battery contained two troops referred to as A and B for D Battery and C and D for J Battery. The Troops of M Battery were known as M (Madras) and J (Java) commemorating the battery's formation and first battle respectively. All batteries of Royal Horse Artillery regiments were identified by letters of the alphabet unlike other artillery units which were numbered.

Although most accounts state that the regiment's OP tanks were Shermans, photographic evidence shows that at least one Cromwell was on hand with M Battery in early 1945 and this is depicted on page 23 of the Camouflage and Markings section of this book.

5th Regiment Royal Horse Artillery.
Made up of G, K and CC Batteries, the regiment was attached to 7th Armoured Division. G Battery was referred to as Mercer's Troop in recognition of the initiative and courage shown by its commander, Captain Cavalië Mercer, at Waterloo in 1815 and was made up of A and B Troops. K (Hondeghem) Battery joined 7th Armoured Division during the

early days of the North African campaign and contained D and E/F Troops. The name commemorates its participation in the defence of the village of Hondeghem, about 20 kilometres south of Dunkirk, in late May 1940 against an overwhelming German force supported by tanks and dive bombers. Today the main street of Hondeghem is known as Rue de la Ker Battery.

Formed after the 1940 French campaign CC Battery, with C and H Troops, served with the division throughout the battles in North Africa and Italy. In North-western Europe CC Battery most often supported 1st Royal Tank Regiment and as the junior formation of 5th Royal Horse Artillery was often given the task of leading the regiment in order to gain its Battle Honours.

In February and March 1944 the regiment was outfitted with Sexton self-propelled guns and Cromwell OP tanks in order to keep pace with the division's armour. Supporting the tanks of 22nd Armoured Brigade the regiment most famously took part in the actions around Villers-Bocage in June 1944 and the subsequent Battle of the Brigade Box where the Sextons fired over open sights at the advancing Germans. Following the great advances made after the battles around Falaise, the regiment took part in the liberation of

....text continued on page 51

Photographed south-east of Caen in late July 1944, this heavily camouflaged Cromwell Mk IV OP tank of 5th Royal Horse Artillery can be identified by the combined formation badge of 7th Armoured Division and white unit serial number just visible to the left of the WD Number. These markings are also discussed on page 23 of the Camouflage and Markings section. Note the driver's diagonally-split hatch. With the introduction of the Type F hull these diagonal models were retro-fitted to many older hulls.

SELF-PROPELLED ARTILLERY REGIMENT, JUNE 1944

Unfortunately, accurate records of actual vehicle strengths for the regiments of the Royal Artillery have not survived the war and what information we have is largely based on photographic evidence and unit war diaries. The War Establishment (WE) directives issued in early 1944 provided for Artillery Observation Post (AOP) tanks to be allocated to Medium, Self-propelled, Field and Royal Horse Artillery regiments. The tanks were held at regimental, battery and troop command level in all except the self-propelled units where the battery commanders were transported in cars. The batteries were divided into what were referred to as an 'O' Party, which operated in the forward area, and a 'G' Party which was based with the guns. The specialist AOP tanks were fitted with two Number 19 and two Number 38 wireless sets, the latter a portable model. The main gun was retained and often used in combat by some units to 'pin' a target until the batteries could concentrate their fire. These vehicles should not be confused with the command version of the Cromwell which was usually allocated to headquarters units of armoured divisions or regiments. These command tanks had an additional large wireless set situated in the gunner's position and the tank's main weapon was replaced with a wooden dummy. By far the most common basis for the AOP conversion was the US M4 Medium tank and the units which operated these are recorded in some detail in the second book in this series, Sherman Tanks: British Army and Royal Marines, Normandy Campaign 1944. Both field artillery regiments attached to 7th Armoured Division, 3rd Royal Horse Artillery and 5th Royal Horse Artillery, were equipped with Cromwell AOP tanks and the diagram presented here is based on those formations. Within the British army the usual policy was not to mix vehicle types but both these regiments are known to have also operated a number of Sherman tanks and one is shown in our photograph at right. The markings of this tank clearly identify a battery commander, suggesting that the regiment was organised, perhaps unofficially, using elements of the orders specifically issued for RHA regiments and self-propelled units. Even so, the allocation of tanks to the battery commanders would mean an increase of three to any official allocation and the fact that the barrel is an obvious wooden dummy may indicate that this tank came from a Royal Armoured Corps unit. The Royal Artillery tactical signs shown here would apply to any Field or Medium artillery formation. The regiments of the RHA numbered their batteries in a unique sequence and their tactical signs usually incorporated the battery letter. A few artillery units were equipped with OP tanks based on the Cavalier Mk I and like the command tanks, these were fitted with wooden dummy guns. An example of a Cavalier AOP is shown in the colour illustration on page 17.

Above: The Sherman V OP tank of Major Dennis Wells, commander of K Battery, 5th Royal Horse Artillery, destroyed during the fighting for Villers-Bocage in July 1944. The tactical sign identifying the commander of an artillery regiment's second battery is clearly visible on the driver's hood. The unit serial number of 76 denotes the second field regiment in an armoured division. Note the wooden dummy gun in the foreground.

| **REGIMENTAL HEADQUARTERS** |  | | **Light Aid Detachment REME** | **Headquarters Signals Section** |

Regimental Commander

The organisation shown here is based on War Establishment (WE) II/190A/2, Field (S.P.) Regiment, RA (25-pdr RAM) dated 25 May 1944.

1st Battery

Battery Commander

Although a Sherman OP is shown here the battery headquarters was officially allocated a 5 cwt car and a 15 cwt wireless lorry.

2nd Battery

Second and third batteries as for first battery.

3rd Battery

| **A Troop** | **B Troop** | **C Troop** | **D Troop** | **E Troop** | **F Troop** |

'O' Party    'O' Party    'O' Party   'O' Party   'O' Party   'O' Party

RA | RB | RC | RD | RE | RF

A Troop Commander | *A Troop Commander* | *A Troop Commander* | *A Troop Commander* | *A Troop Commander* | *A Troop Commander*

'G' Party   'G' Party   'G' Party   'G' Party    'G' Party   'G' Party

GA | GB | GC | GD | GE | GF

A Troop Subaltern | *A Troop Subaltern* | *A Troop Subaltern* | *A Troop Subaltern* | *A Troop Subaltern* | *A Troop Subaltern*

Full colour versions of the tactical signs used by the Royal Artillery are shown in the Camouflage and Markings section of this book which begins on page 17.

..............................text continued from page 49

Ghent in early September 1944. One of the regiment's last actions took place in early May 1945 when the Sextons of G Battery reached the Elbe river and immediately brought a German cruiser and merchant ship under fire, causing considerable damage.

13th (The Honourable Artillery Company) Regiment Royal Horse Artillery. Made up of G, H and I Batteries, this regiment was attached to 11th Armoured Division in June 1944. The regiment was equipped with Sherman OP tanks until late February 1945 when they were replaced by Cromwells.

The author and historian Patrick Delaforce, who served with the division, was adamant that some tanks at least were armed and actually fired their guns in anger against German armour.

53rd (Worcester Yeomanry) Airlanding Light (AL) Regiment, RA. Specially trained to support 6th Airborne Division during the Normandy landings the regiment contained 210, 211 and 212 Batteries.

On 21 June 1944 a number of Centaurs

Taken from the Royal Marine Armoured Support Group were received and allocated to X Troop of 210 Battery and S Troop of 212 Battery. The regiment's diary is quite clear on the origin of the tanks, the date of delivery and how they were initially utilised. The exact number received is not recorded but if the reference to 'two Troops' is correct it may have been as many as twelve (1).

In early August, due to the severe manpower shortage, the regiment's armoured batteries were disbanded.

In order to utilise the Centaurs and continue to support 6th Airborne Division the formation of a battery made up of Canadian troops was authorised and on 6 August 1st Canadian Centaur Battery, under the command of Major D.W.M. Cooper, took control of the remaining tanks.

Surviving Canadian 1st Army documents clearly state that twelve operational Centaurs together with their ammunition supply were available on Friday, 4 August 1944 when the plan was first put forward. A number of British officers and other

Notes

1. Canadian accounts actually confirm the number as twelve.

Command by Lieutenant-Colonel R.B.T. 'Tony' Daniell, a veteran of the desert battles, this Cromwell IV is based on a Type F hull. Note the brace on the turret front used to hold the dummy gun in place. The markings applied to OP tanks and aspects of this tank are discussed in detail on page 23 of the Camouflage and Markings section.

Photographed in Süstedt, south of Bremen, in April 1945, the markings of this OP tank identify the commanding officer of 5th Royal Horse Artillery, the second senior artillery regiment of 7th Armoured Division. This tank and its markings are discussed in detail on page 23 of the Camouflage and Markings section.

ranks stayed with the battery which remained under the control of 53rd Airlanding Light Regiment until 19 August 1944.

The diary of the British regiment continued to refer to the battery for some time as 'X Battery' and this has been the cause of some confusion in post-war accounts. Indeed, the Canadian connection is not mentioned until 19 August, the day the battery was detached from the regiment, when the 'Canadian Centaur Bty (X Armd Bty)' is acknowledged for the first time.

It is nothing short of miraculous that any of the Centaurs had been kept running and on 22 August 1944 five vehicles were abandoned due to mechanical failures and two days later the battery reported that just one Sherman, two Centaurs and a single Cromwell were on hand, the latter borrowed from the 6th Airborne Reconnaissance Regiment.

Towards the end of the month the Airborne Division was withdrawn from the front line and the 1st Canadian Centaur Battery was disbanded. The last tanks were handed to 259th Armoured Delivery Squadron.

151st (Ayrshire Yeomanry) Field Artillery Regiment. Attached to 11th Armoured Division in June 1944, the regiment was equipped with Sherman OP tanks until March 1945 when they were replaced by Cromwells. This coincided with the issue of the new Comet tank to the division's armoured regiments.

The author and historian Patrick Delaforce, in his history of the division, recounts that the OP tanks were often called upon to fire their guns in battle and, on at least one occasion, duelled with German tanks (1).

65th (Highland) Medium Regiment, RA. Made up of 222 and 223 Batteries the regiment was equipped with a number of Cavalier AOP tanks in early 1944. Parts of the regiment landed in France on D-Day near Courselles-sur-Mer and throughout the Normandy campaign supported 6th Airborne Division and 51st (Highland) Division. The regiment served in North-west Europe until the end of the war and was disbanded in 1947.

Notes

1. Delaforce served with 11th Armoured Division during the war and his accounts are often based on his personal experiences and recollections.

As originally envisaged, this unit was raised as a purely assault formation, made up older Centaur tanks with their engines removed to allow for extra ammunition stowage. The tanks would be carried towards the Normandy beaches on modified Landing Craft, Tank (LCT) giving fire support to the infantry on the shore.

However, in early February 1944, while watching an exercise involving the Centaurs, King George VI asked when the tanks would land and was informed that they would not as they had no engines. Standing nearby, General Montgomery ordered that the engines be replaced immediately, rightly concerned that these immobile tanks might block the invasion beaches in the first crucial hours of the operation.

By 21 February the engines had been refitted, twenty Sherman tanks had been found for the troop commanders and what had been known as the Support Craft Regiment was renamed the Royal Marines Armoured Support Group. At first it was decided that the tanks would advance just 200 metres from the shoreline but this was increased to 2,000 metres in late March 1944. Consisting of 1st Royal Marine Armoured Support Regiment, 2nd Royal Marine Armoured Support Regiment and 5th Royal Marine (Independent) Armoured Support Battery the tanks of the Royal Marines Armoured Support Group (RMASG) remained in the front line for almost three weeks until the surviving Centaurs were finally passed on to 53rd Airlanding Light Regiment and from there to 1st Canadian Centaur Battery (1).

The two regiments were each made up of two batteries, numbered from 1 to 4 and each battery contained four troops which were referred to as A, B, C and D for 1st Battery, E, F, G and H for 2nd Battery, P, Q, S and T for 3rd Battery and W, X, Y and Z for 4th Battery. The four troops of the independent 5th Battery were designated R, S, T and V Troops. From the available photographs it appears that each tank was named to correspond with the troop letter.

Each troop contained four Centaurs and a Sherman OP tank giving a total of twenty Sherman and eighty Centaur tanks for the entire group. Each troop was divided into a Left Section and a Right Section,

Notes

1. A number were also handed over to the French 13.Regiment de Dragons, however, this only accounts for the Centaurs. What became of the Sherman OP tanks remains a mystery.

A Centaur Mk IV of H Troop, 2nd Battery, Royal Marine Armoured Support Group, photographed during the second week of June 1944. Interestingly, the commander is wearing a black Royal Armoured Corps beret with the badge of the Royal Tank Regiment, while the beret of the crewman sitting on the left side trackguard has the badge of the Royal Marines. The tanks of the Royal Marine Armoured Support Group and their markings are discussed in detail on pages 19 and 20.

Left: A Centaur Mk IV of 1st Battery photographed in Britain just prior to the invasion. A piece of colour film exists of this tank which suggests that it was roughly repainted in SCC 15 in a similar fashion to the tank shown on page 20.

At right: Photographed on 13 June 1944 near Tilly-sur-Seulles, south-east of Bayeux, this Centaur Mk IV is from 2nd Battery, 1st Armoured Support Regiment. Scraped together from various sources most of these Royal Marine Centaurs were probably finished in Standard Camouflage Colour (SCC) 2 Brown rather than SCC 15 Olive Drab which was not introduced until April 1944. Exceptions almost certainly existed and these and the markings of the Royal Marines discussed in detail on pages 19 and 20 of the Camouflage and Markings section of this book.

each of two Centaurs and both sections were controlled by the troop commander from a Sherman tank. Each section was transported on a Landing Craft, Tank (Assault) (LCT(A)) with two Centaurs positioned side by side at the front and the Sherman OP of the troop commander behind them. An ammunition team of one NCO and four ammunition handlers was included in each vessel and some of these teams remained with the tanks after 6 June, although most returned to England. The group, regiment and battery headquarters had no tanks, their purpose being to command and to ensure an adequate supply of ammunition.

Overall command of the RMASG was exercised by Brigadier D.C.W. Sanders, an artillery officer, while his deputy was Colonel A.J. Harvey of the Royal Marines. A number of officers and gunner-drivers were seconded from the Royal Artillery and maintenance and repairs were carried out by fitters and mechanics from the Royal Armoured Corps. The majority of the crews were, however, Royal Marine gunners.

On 6 June, the tanks of the 5th Battery supported the units assaulting Sword beach with sixteen Centaur and four Sherman OP tanks. All the tanks were ashore by the early hours of the following morning with the exception of two Centaurs and a single Sherman whose landing craft returned to England with the tanks on board. The 2nd Support Regiment with twenty-six Centaurs and seven Sherman tanks landed at least one troop on Juno beach by the evening of the first day. However, one LCT(A) was lost with all its vehicles. The tanks of the 1st Regiment supported the units landing on Gold beach losing a Sherman OP tank to enemy fire as it left its landing craft.

Despite the loss of twenty Centaurs in the Channel crossing and the casualties sustained during the landings, including Brigadier Sanders who was killed, twelve Shermans and forty-eight Centaurs were ashore by mid-morning and engaging enemy positions. By the end of the following day another twelve Centaurs had been landed.

The markings used by the Royal Marines are described and shown in the illustration section on pages 19 and 20.

The complex history of the design and evolution of the Cromwell tank and its predecessors, the A 24 Cavalier and the A27L Centaur, is a story of indecision exacerbated by conflicting interests and overlapping areas of responsibility. The development of the hull types, armament and turret proceeded for the most part independently, making classification confusing and complicated. The identification of a tank as, for example, a Centaur Mk I or a Cromwell Mk IV is dependent on the hull type, turret and armament and listed in this section are the main characteristics of each.

The reader should note that I have purposely excluded some internal changes as these were for the most part minor and would in any case not help in classifying a particular tank from period photographs.

The bolted turret originally designed for the Cavalier remained basically unchanged with the only major modification being the incorporation of an All Round Vision (ARV) commander's cupola in 1944. These were, however, comparatively rare. In the Cromwell turret the commander and gunner were provided with rotating and pivoting periscopes while the earlier commander's cupola, which could be rotated, was also fitted with episcopes (1). Pistol ports were installed on both sides of the turret towards the rear. A Besa 7.92mm machine gun was mount coaxially with the main gun and a 2in Mk I* Bombthrower was fixed into the turret roof to fire forward. The main armament was initially the Ordnance Quick Firing (OQF) 6 pdr Mk III or Mk V gun but requests for a more powerful weapon which also had a high explosive capability led to the introduction of the OQF 75mm with the Centaur Mk III and Cromwell Mk IV being the first tanks fitted with the new gun (2).

Possible delays in production were alleviated by the rather ingenious solution of simply reboring existing 6pdr guns to accept the 75mm rounds meaning that the two guns were easily exchanged. The 75mm gun is easily identifiable by its large muzzle brake. The close support versions were of course armed with the 95mm Mk I howitzer.

Notes

1. The official vehicle manual refers to all as periscopes although the difference is significant.

2. Although the 6pdr gun's armour-piercing ability was greatly increased with the introduction of the Sabot round, these were not available in quantity until 1944 when the Cromwell was just about to go into battle.

Photographed in Britain shortly before the Normandy landings these Cavalier Mk I OP tanks are both built on Type B hulls. Of note are the single lockers on the hull side trackguards (1), the bolted-on cover of the machine gun aperture (2) and the early type fenders with rear-view mirror (3). The cone-shaped bolt covers (4) on the turret front and sides were a feature of the Cavalier, Centaur and Cromwell production vehicles. Unusually, both tanks seem to have retained their 6pdr guns. The markings identify 65th (Highland) Medium Regiment, RA and the closest tank is also depicted in the colour illustration on page 17.

Tank Classifications. This list should be read in conjunction with the Hull Types list which follows and compared with the photographs in this section and throughout the book. War Department, or WD, Numbers, where known, have been included under each type heading. These unique numbers Identified a particular vehicle for its complete operational life but it should be noted that different models could have been allocated numbers from the same series or range of numbers meaning that the number in itself does not necessarily denote a particular version.

The Centaur Mk III tanks seen here are all built on Type C hulls and armed with 75mm guns. Note that the machine-gunner's periscope has been deleted and the aperture covered with a metal plate (1). Note also the lack of engine air intakes on the rear deck (2) and the early, perforated tyres of the roadwheels. This image also provides a clear view of the turret spotlight (3) and the protective cover for its lead (4), the turret roof periscopes (5) and the commander's early-type hatch (6). All vehicles seem to have been painted in a base coat of Standard Camouflage Colour (SCC) 2 Brown with a disruptive pattern of SCC 14 Blue-black applied, against regulations, in a soft, mottled scheme.

Photographed in April 1944, just weeks before the Normandy landings, this Centaur Mk I is based on a Type A hull and equipped with a 6pdr gun. The significance of the U suffix to the WD Number, T.183933U, is not understood but can be seen in other photographs of early production Centaur and Cromwell tanks. It may indicate an unarmoured or, more likely, an upgraded tank as other photographs in this series show that this vehicle was fitted with the Cromwell-style air intake on the rear deck.

Cavalier Mk I. Built on both the riveted Type A and Type B hulls this tank was armed with the OQF 6pdr Mk III or Mk V gun and featured a bolted turret and narrow, 355mm tracks. Most Cavaliers that saw service had been converted to Observation Post (OP) tanks. The 6pdr guns of these vehicles were removed and replaced with a wooden dummy. Interestingly a number of Cavaliers were given to the French army in 1945.

Cavalier Mk II. A single example of this version was built as a trial vehicle. It was almost identical to the Cavalier Mk I with the exception of the wider 394mm tracks.

Centaur Mk I. Fitted with the OQF 6pdr Mk III or, more commonly, Mk V gun this tank was built with the Type A, B and C riveted hulls. The turret was essentially the same as that fitted to the Cavalier Mk I and the tracks were the standard 355mm models. Some tanks built with the Type A hull were allocated WD Numbers from the series T130120 - 130164 while all those based on the Type B and C, with the remainder of the Type A hulls, were numbered in the range T183800-186510. The pilot models were numbered from T171762-171766. Although well over 1,000 of these tanks were built, most were used in training or other non-combat roles.

Centaur Mk II. This model was identical to the Centaur Mk I with the exception of the wider 394mm tracks as used with the Cavalier Mk II and the deletion of the hull machine gun. There is no available information on which type of hull was used and only a single experimental vehicle was built.

Centaur Mk III. Armed with the OQF 75mm Mk V gun these vehicles were built with the Type C and D riveted hulls and featured 355mm tracks. From 1943 many Centaur Mk I vehicles were upgraded to Mk III configuration by the addition of the 75mm gun. A total of 233 were produced and a number were converted to close support and anti-aircraft tanks. Centaur Mk III tanks built on the Type C hull were allocated WD Numbers between T217801-217880.

Centaur Mk IV. This tank was essentially a Centaur Mk III fitted with the 95mm howitzer. In 1944 a number were fitted with deep wading gear and waterproofing and were operated by the Royal Marine Armoured Support Group. These were the only Centaurs known to have been used in a combat role. A number of Centaur Mk IV tanks were also converted into combat dozers by the MG Car Company.

Cromwell Mk I. Armed with the OQF 6pdr Mk III or Mk V gun these tanks were built on the Type A and Type C riveted hulls. The turret was bolted and the tracks were the 355mm width variety. Production ended with the introduction of the Cromwell Mk IV equipped with the 75mm gun and just 357 Mk I vehicles were built. WD Numbers allocated to vehicles based on the Type A hulls were taken from the series T121150-121406 while those built on Type C hulls fell with the ranges T120415-120689, T188657-188681 and T121150-121406.

Cromwell Mk II. Built by Vauxhall on a riveted hull which was similar to the Type B, this tank was armed with the 6pdr Mk III gun. The wide tracks were the same as those fitted to the Centaur Mk II and the gun was installed in a composite turret which featured both cast and welded components and was very similar to that used on the Churchill Mk VII. The Cromwell II did not enter production. A similar trial vehicle built on the riveted Type A hull was referred to as Pilot D.

Cromwell Mk III. This tank was actually a newly-built Centaur Mk I fitted with a Meteor V12 engine. Armed with the OQF 6pdr Mk III or Mk V gun just 200 were built due to the unavailability of suitable Centaurs. The Cromwell Mk III was built on both the Type A and C hulls.

Cromwell Mk IV. Like the Cromwell Mk III this version was also a Centaur, in this case a Mk III, fitted with a Meteor engine. All vehicles were armed with the OQF 75mm Mk V or Mk Va gun and were built on the Type C, D, E and F hulls. Later Cromwell IV tanks saw the

....text continued on page 60

Photographed in Britain in late April 1944, these Centaur Mk IV tanks are from 5th (Independent) Armoured Support Battery, Royal Marine Armoured Support Group. The absence of the machine-gunner's periscope (1) identifies the hull of the tank in the foreground as an early Type C. Note that the machine-gun aperture has been blanked off (2), as it was with all the Marines Centaur tanks, and that the cover for the No. 19 dial sight (3) appears to have been painted white. Just visible is the name Margaret, painted inside the open driver's visor (4). The distinctive markings of this vehicle are also shown and discussed in the Camouflage and Markings section on page 19.

This Cromwell Mk VI of 2nd Fife and Forfar Yeomanry, based on what is probably a Type C hull, provides a good view of the exhaust cowl (1), smoke emitters (2), tow coupling (3) and final drive (4). The ammunition boxes welded to the trackguards (5) provided extra stowage and were a common field modification. This photograph was taken at the crossing of the Weser near Petershagen in Germany on 7 April 1945.

This image provides a clear view of the driver's vision port, shown here in the completely opened position (5). The port contained a smaller wicket door which could be opened outwards and behind the door was an armoured glass block. Note that the glass is missing here, as it is in many contemporary photographs. It was held in place by the bracket (6) at the lower inside edge and could be removed by raising the round catch (7) at the centre of the top inside edge of the port. The glass very quickly gathered dirt and dust and was probably dispensed with in many instances. Note the two periscopes (8) in front of the driver's hatch on the hull roof which is partly opened (9).

text continued from page 58

Notes

1) See the introduction for an explanation of the Final Specification.

introduction of the Final Specification (1) of February 1944 which upgraded some features from Centaur to Cromwell standard. These tanks were sometimes referred to as the Battle Cromwell. At about this time an All Round Vision (ARV) cupola, a vane sight and smoke emitters were incorporated into production on all hull types as the parts became available. In addition, solid Avon tyres replaced the earlier perforated models on the road wheels, although these could still be seen until the end of the war. This was the most numerous version of the Cromwell built with over 1,935 vehicles leaving the production lines. Cromwell IV tanks based on the Type F Hull were allocated WD Numbers from the series T188687-188926 while those based on the Type D and E hulls used numbers taken from the range T187501-188082.

Cromwell Mk V. Very similar in appearance to the Cromwell Mk IV, these vehicles were built to the Final Specification on a Type C hull and armed with the OQF 75mm Mk V gun. Versions built on welded hulls were referred to as Mk VwD and Mk VwE and the former was fitted with applique armour.

Cromwell Mk VI. This version was the close support model of the Cromwell and was one of the most successful variants, although just 341 vehicles were built. Based on the Type C, D, E and F hulls the Cromwell Mk VI was armed with the 95mm Mk I howitzer in place of the 75mm gun. Cromwell VI tanks were allocated WD Numbers from within the ranges T188657-188681 and T187501-188082.

Cromwell VII. This model was an upgrade of the Cromwell Mk IV, Mk V and Mk VI tanks armed with the 75mm Mk V or Mk Va gun and built using the Type C, D, E and F hulls with the wider 394mm tracks, although none had applique armour. The Cromwell VII was manufactured very late in the war, with some sources suggesting that production was post-1945, and few were used in combat. The versions built on the Type Dw and Type Ew welded hulls were referred to as Cromwell Mk VIIwD and Cromwell VIIwE respectively. The welded hull tanks were allocated WD Numbers from the series T121701-121822.

Cromwell VIII. Built on the Type D, E and F hulls this tank followed the same specification as the Cromwell Mk VII but was armed with the 95mm Mk I howitzer.

Cromwell Mk X. An existing Centaur Mk I fitted with a Meteor engine for trials. Armed with the OQF 6pdr Mk III or Mk V gun these tanks were built on the Type A or C hull. The exact number built is uncertain, with at least one authoritative source suggesting that a single vehicle based on a Type A hull was completed. It is known, however, that any WD Numbers were taken from the range T171762-171766.

Photographed in Hamburg during the afternoon of 3 May 1945, this Cromwell Mk VI of C Squadron, 1st Royal Tank Regiment is built on what may be a welded Type Dw hull with the single periscope over the driver's position (1), although it does not seem to have been fitted with applique armour. Note that the opened driver's port has the glass block in place (2). The squared-off lower portion of the 95mm gun's counterweight is also clearly visible here (3). The vehicle in the foreground is also depicted in the colour illustration on page 24.

Hull Types. During the development and production of the Cavalier, Centaur and Cromwell an astonishing number of modifications were made to the hull and while many of these were minor, some were significant, such as the adoption of welding in place of riveting in the assembly process. The major hull types are listed below.

Type A. This was the first version as seen on the Cavalier Mk I with top opening hatches for the driver and hull machine-gunner, an escape hatch in the tank's floor plate, four lockers along the hull sides and a layered floor plate of 6 to 8mm thickness. A 7.92mm Besa machine gun in a No. 20 gimbal mount was fitted into the front glacis. A No. 35 periscopic gun sight was provided for the machine gun and the gunner also had a periscope in the hull roof in front of his hatch. The air intake on the engine deck was fitted to all Cromwells and, depending on the manufacturer, was optional on Centaurs. This hull was riveted and was used on the Cavalier Mk I, Centaur Mk I, Cromwell Mk I, Mk III and Mk X.

Type B. This version was very similar to the Type A and was also riveted but the hull machine-gunner's hatch now opened to the left side and his periscope was deleted. In addition there were now just three stowage lockers. This hull was used with the Cavalier Mk I and Centaur Mk I.

Type C. This existed in both an early and late version and both were similar to the Type B. The sole initial change was a reduction in the thickness of the armour on the engine compartment to compensate for the increases in weight brought about by the many earlier modifications. As this was of course purely an internal change these hulls are difficult to identify in photographs. The later model saw the re-introduction of the hull machine-gunner's periscope and new-style trackguards. Both versions had the new air intake and either the No. 20 or No. 21 mount for the hull machine gun. Both hulls were used with the Centaur Mk I, Mk III and Mk IV and the Cromwell Mk I, Mk III, Mk IV and Mk V.

Type D. Similar to the Type C, this riveted hull featured a redesigned engine deck which allowed easier access to the radiators. The 7.92mm Besa hull machine gun used the No. 21 ball mounting and the gunner's periscope and the trackguards were altered. This hull was used for the Centaur Mk III, Centaur Mk IV, the Cromwell Mk IV and Mk VI.

....*text continued on page 63*

Photographed in Hamburg on 5 May 1945, this Cromwell and Challenger are both from B Squadron, 8th King's Royal Irish Hussars. This Cromwell Mk IV is built on a Type F hull identified by the side-opening driver's hatch (1) and the single locker on each side of the hull (2). The turret stowage boxes (3), covered here in what appear to be German Zeltbahn camouflage tent quarters, and commander's vane sight (4) were standard fixtures on the Type F and also were retro-fitted to many older hulls.

The photograph at the top of the page was taken in Normandy and shows a Cromwell Mk IV. The opened driver's hatch in the background (1) and the periscope above the machine-gunner's position (2) would suggest that this may be a later production Type C hull. Also visible is the machine-gunner's hatch in the open position (3), the left side locker and its latches (4) and the Avon solid-tyre roadwheels (5). The image at left depicts a Cromwell Mk IV of 8th King's Royal Irish Hussars and this tank is also shown in the Camouflage and Markings section on page 21. Note the opened driver's visor with its glass block in place (6) and the All Round Vision (ARV) cupola (7) also shown in detail in our photograph (8), here fitted to a Churchill, and the smoke emitter fixed to the left side trackguard (9). The Churchill tank commander's companion wears the black RAC beret with the badge of the Royal Tank Regiment. Note also that the turret roof of the Cromwell at left has been painted white.

text continued from page..58

Type Dw. This was essentially a welded version of the Type D hull and the introduction of welding to the assembly process was the single most significant modification made during the Cromwell's production life.

The pilot model featured a welded turret but this was not incorporated into production. The welded construction of the hull and the adoption of a single-piece floor plate decreased the overall weight allowing for the addition of applique armour. One of the driver's periscopes was moved to the centre of his roof hatch and the 355mm tracks were retained.

The designation of tanks assembled with welded hulls was suffixed with 'w', for example Crowmell Mk Vw and the vehicle's WD Number, which was usually prominently displayed, also ended with the letter W.

Type E. These were almost identical to the Type D riveted hull with the exception of an increase in the armoured thickness of the floor plate which was now made from a single metal sheet. They are therefore very difficult to differentiate in photographs. These hulls were used to assemble both the Cromwell Mk IV and Mk VI models.

Type Ew. Other than the lack of rivets, the only difference between this hull and the Type E was an alteration in the final drive. The Type Ew hull retained the 355mm tracks and was used with the Cromwell Mk V. A later version was fitted with heavy duty front axles and the wider, 394mm tracks and used on the Cromwell VII. With both versions the completed tank's designation included the letters w and E, for example Cromwell VwE. It should be noted that this hull was not fitted with applique armour as the welded Type D version was.

Type F. The final design, this hull was very similar to the Type E. Changes included side-opening doors for both the driver and hull machine-gunner. This meant that the hull trackguards could now only accommodate two lockers and to compensate two stowage bins were added to the turret sides. A towing cable was carried on the glacis and on later versions a WD Pattern sprung towbar was added.

All Type F hulls were built with Cromwell suspension as standard. This type of hull was used on the Cromwell Mk IV and Mk VI.

This photograph, taken during Operation Epsom in late June 1944, offers a comparison between the Cromwell in the foreground and the Centaur following behind. Both are externally very similar, with the most obvious differences being the main gun and the trackguards. While Observation (OP) tanks based on the Cromwell retained their main gun, and often used it, the 6pdr of the Centaur was removed and replaced with a wooden dummy. The commander's hatches on both tanks have been fitted with field-modified metal frames to hold maps and other documents.

Tamiya Inc
Shizuoka City, Japan
www.tamiya.com

Airfix
www.airfix.com/uk-en/

Revell
www.revell.com/

Panzer Art
Ul. Borowa 7
Slawkow
Poland
www.panzerart.pl

Italeri S.p.A.
Via Pradazzo 6/b
40012 Calderara di Reno, Bologna,
Italy
www.italeri.com

Jordi Rubio
Carrer de Còrsega, 625, 08025 Barcelona,
Spain
www. Jordirubio.com/en

Star Decals
www.star-decals.net
Formerly Bison Decals

SKP Models
Tribrichy 47
537 01 Chrudim
Czech republic
www.skpmodel.eu

Armourfast
103 High Street Walkern
Hertfordshire
SG2 7NU. United Kingdom
www.armourfast.com

Hauler
Jan Sobotka
Moravská 38
620 00 Brno
Czech Republic
www.hauler.cz

Voyager Model
Room 501, No.411 4th Village
SPC Jinshan District
Shanghai 200540
P.R.China
www.voyagermodel.com

Aber
ul. Jalowcowa 15, 40-750 Katowice,
Poland
www.aber.net.pl

Friulmodel
H 8142. Urhida, Nefelejcs u. 2., Hungary
www.friulmodel.hu

Modelkasten
Chiyoda-ku Kanda, Nishiki-Cho 1-7, Tokyo,
Japan
www.modelkasten.com
Very difficult to navigate but worthwhile

S & S Models
22 Briar Close
Burnham on Sea
Somerset TA 1HU
United Kingdom
www.sandsmodels.com

M Workshop Singapore
91 Bencoolen St Sunshine Plaza01-58
Singapore
www.themworkshop.com

ROCHM Model
www.rochmmodel.com
rochmmodel@gmail.com

Eduard Model Accessories
Mirova 170, 435 21 Obrnice
Czech Republic
www.eduard.com

RB Model
Powstancow Wlkp.29B
64-360 Zbaszyn
Poland
www.rbmodel.com

Black Dog
Petr Polanka
Letecká 549
Libèice nad Vltavou 252 66,
Czech Republic
www.blackdog.cz

Dan Taylor Modelworks
55 Town Hill,
West Malling,
Kent, ME19 6QL
United Kingdom
www.dantaylormodelworks.com

Accurate Armour
Kelburn Business Park,
Port Glasgow PA14 6TD,
United Kingdom
www.accurate-armour.com

Milicast
9 Rannoch Street, Battlefield
Glasgow G44 4DF
United Kingdom
www.milicast.com

In researching and compiling the unit histories and markings chapters of this book I relied heavily on the works of B.T. White, John Sandars and the studies into the camouflage colours employed by the British army published by Michael Starmer. Although Mr. White and Mr. Sandars are sadly no longer with us and their books were published some time ago, they are still some of the most easily accessible references available. Over the years I have also compiled a great deal of information gleaned from memoirs and unit diaries which although far too numerous to mention here should be at least acknowledged. Much of the technical information was based on the work of David Fletcher and the instruction manuals issued by the Chief Inspector of Fighting Vehicles during the war. All the illustrations were based on photographs of actual tanks and where I have been forced to speculate I have tried to make this clear. I would like to thank the modellers who graciously allowed me to publish the images of their work and Rupert Harding and Stephen Chumbley, my editors at Pen & Sword, for their advice and assistance and for allowing me to bring my work to a large audience. Of the product manufacturers I must make special mention of Roberto Reale of Royal Model, Sheng Hui of ROCHM, Jan Zdiarsky from Eduard Accessories who all helped enormously. I would particularly like to thank Ian Carter, the curator of the Imperial War Museum photographic archive. As always, I am indebted to Karl Berne, Valeri Polokov and J.Howard Parker for their invaluable assistance with the photographs and period insignia.

ALSO AVAILABLE IN THE TANKCRAFT SERIES

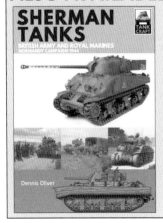

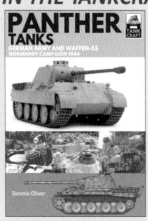

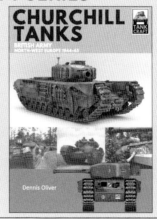

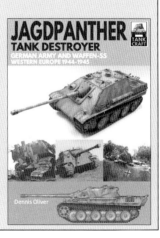